The
Politics of Literacy

The
Politics of Literacy

Edited by Martin Hoyles

Writers and Readers Publishing Cooperative

Published 1977 by Writers and Readers Publishing Cooperative,
14, Talacre Road, London NW5 3PE.

Set and made up by Jetset, Carlton House, Great Queen Street,
London WC2.

Printed and bound in Great Britain by Redwood Burn Ltd.,
Trowbridge and Esher.

Contents

Preface 5

1 **History and Ideology 9**
Introduction 10
The History and Politics of Literacy, *Martin Hoyles* 14
Education: Programmes and People, *Quintin Hoare* 33

2 **Class and Culture 55**
Introduction 56
Extract from The Conditions of the Working Class in England, *Friedrich Engels, 1845* 59
A Worker Questions History, *Bertolt Brecht* 62
Class and Art, *Leon Trotsky* 63
Literature Will be Scrutinised, *Bertolt Brecht* 67

3 **The Meaning of Literacy 69**
Introduction 70
Properly Literate, *Wayne O'Neil* 73
In Praise of Learning, *Bertolt Brecht* 78
Experience of Literacy in Working Class Life, *Peggy Temple* 79
An Open Letter 86

4 **Sexism 89**
Introduction 90
Boys will be boys but what will girls be?
Camilla Nightingale 95
Memoirs of a Suffragette, *June Kingston* 99
Sexist Bias in Reading Schemes, *Glenys Lobban* 103

Does it really matter whether a man desire another man? 111

Word Consciousness: Sexist Language and Attitudes, *Kristine L Falco* 114

5 Racism 125

Introduction 126

Three Poems on Racism, *Inderjit Randhawa* 132

All Things White and Beautiful, *Box Dixon* 134

Concerning the Colour of One's Skin, *Harry Sansum* 151

African Vernacular Writing, *Daniel P. Kunene* 153

My Autobiography, *Phillip Christian* 164

6 Class and the Classroom 167

Introduction 168

The Plum Tree, *Bertolt Brecht* 171

Cultural Deprivation and Compensatory Education, *Martin Hoyles* 172

Well, I mean, he had the chance didn't he? *Craig Paice* 182

Beyond the Classroom Walls, *Ken Worpole* 186

Two Poems on inequality, *Christine Reed* 200

Out There or Where the Masons Went, *Harold Rosen* 202

Preface

The questions this book poses and discusses are clearly political ones: literacy for whom? in what way? and for what purpose? Hence its title — *The Politics of Literacy.*

Of course, literacy is news today. Literacy has made headlines. 'Standards are falling', says one; 'rising', says another. The very terms being used, 'standards', 'values', should serve to warn us that the fate of education has been linked to the fate of sterling. Monetary value. The gold standard . . . Education seems less a current issue than one of currency!

What 'values' must education forego in the rush for economic recovery?

1976 saw the call for a 'great national debate'. But what is at stake? Who is conducting it? and for whose benefit? Prime Minister James Callaghan in his speech delivered at Ruskin College, Oct. 18th, 1976, declared that 'to be basically literate' is one of the main aims of education. 'To the teachers I would say that you must satisfy the parents and industry that what you are doing meets their requirements and the needs of their children.' But where is the reference — from a Labour Prime Minister — to the needs of the Labour movement? the trade unions? the working class?

Or is the 'great debate' just another smoke-screen? Does it mean a bankrupt and iniquitous system will be rescued by social engineers and bureaucrats? Can we seriously hope for anything positive or enlightened from such quarters?

Political decisions do affect literacy. What will come down to us from 'high places' is the treatment of illiteracy as an isolated malfunction shorn of its political implications. Rather, it is the everyday experience of what is *done* to us, in the name of the GNP and other such abstract standards, that reveals the consequences.

The aim of this book is to re-introduce to the discussion of literacy precisely the suppressed, wider implications. What are the motives which order the use of language in specific social instances? Each section of the book, guided by this fundamental question, sets literacy squarely in its proper perspective. History, ideology, class and culture, sex and race. These are the contexts, the relationships and practical connections examined. These too are the areas of 'cultural silence' usually left unprobed in other discussions of the meaning of literacy. Indeed, the meaning of literacy is cultural. But that is wrongly taken in its restricted, elitist sense. Paulo Freire has tried to open our eyes to the unrestricted sense of cultural literacy:

> Speaking of the word is not a true act if it is not at the same time associated with the right of self-expression and world-expression, of creating and re-creating, of deciding and choosing and ultimately participating in society's historical process.

This is a book which springs originally from experience — that of teaching in London secondary schools, and also of preparing courses for London teachers. Both in its emphasis and purpose, the book is directed to them, as well as all other people who wish to share actively in 'society's historical process'.

This is a 'reader' — a collection of basic texts on cultural literacy. It contains essays, extracts and articles by some well and lesser known writers, some poems by Bertolt Brecht, and other pieces by secondary school students. Individual chapters are equipped with useful bibliographical references and suggestions for further readings.

Richard Appignanesi

Part One

History
and Ideology

Introduction

In the six hundred pages of the Bullock Report there is no attempt to place literacy in a historical context; and there is virtually no reference to any country other than our own.(1) It is in the belief that literacy cannot be understood until it is seen in historical perspective that we start with an article on this subject. Similarly, a world-wide context is necessary — and this is why in this book there are continual references to literacy in other countries.

This historical approach leads to the need to locate educational and cultural ideas in their social context — hence the discussion of ideology in Quintin Hoare's 'Education: Programmes and People'. Hoare provides a framework within which the educational ideologies in this country can be examined. Here, a brief look at the ideology of English teaching, with reference to Hoare's categories, might be illuminating.

Although there is an attempt by some writers on the teaching of English to see it as catering for the needs of industrial society (2) (Hoare's 'Rationalizers'), the main theoretical emphasis in modern English teaching is against such a society. Fred Inglis traces the influence of F.R. Leavis ('Conservative') and David Holbrook ('Romantic') on English teachers:

> These teachers have taught the primacy of the individual sensibility, the unflinching need to keep your private self your own and clear, spontaneous, intelligible, and full of life. They have carried forward such teaching with some antique conceptual weaponry, picked up from Wordsworth here and J.S. Mill there, but it is more than historical accident that its ideology has suggested a mode of dissent from late capitalist and industrial society and a purchase point for the individual sensibility upon the smooth, impassive surfaces of technology.(3)

Leavis's opposition to industrial society is clear in his admiration of Dickens' 'Hard Times' which attacks the degradation and oppression inflicted by industrialism on the machine-hands of Coketown. For Leavis, the main point is that art is destroyed:

> 'The Horse-riding, frowned upon as frivolous and wasteful by Gradgrind and malignantly scorned by Bounderby, brings the machine-hands of Coketown (the spirit-quenching hideousness of which is hauntingly evoked) what they are starved of. It brings to them, not merely amusement, but art, and the spectacle of triumphant activity that, seeming to contain its end within itself, is, in its easy mastery, joyously self-justified. In investing a travelling circus with this kind of symbolic value, Dickens expresses a profounder reaction to industrialism than might have been expected of him. It is not only pleasure and relaxation the Coketowners stand in need of; he feels the dreadful degradation of life that would remain even if they were to be given a forty-four-hour week, comfort, security, and fun.'(4)

There is some similarity between this position and that of Marx who also thought the capitalist mode of production was 'essentially unpropitious for the evolution of literature and art'. This is due to the division of labour which is inimical to the principle of humanism,

> which the proletarian struggle for freedom inherited from earlier democratic and revolutionary movements and evolved to a higher qualitative level: the demand for a free development of a many-sided, integrated man. Contrarily, the hostility to art and culture inherent in the capitalist mode of production brings a disintegration of man, a disintegration of the concrete totality into abstract specialisations.(5)

This reaction against industrial society has led English teachers either to a retreat into individualism or to a concern for reform (Hoare's 'Democratic Tradition'). The latter position sees education as an 'agent of social change'.(6) 'Teachers can alter the institutions they belong to by altering their language-habits.'(7) Language enrichment is necessary because 'there is some evidence to suggest that these deprived and disadvantaged children with poor communication may, at a later date, become the aggressive vandals of adolescence.'(8) The state of society can be repaired: 'Perhaps your classes, with the added perception that you will give them, will be able and willing to start to put things right.'(9)

Clearly, Leavis is being followed rather than Marx. (Leavis is considered to have defeated the Marxists in the thirties.) Art — not revolution — can save society. Michael Rosen puts it bluntly in his article on 'Doing Eng. Lit.':

> Eng.Lit. faculties are the institutional forms that propose, maintain and express an ethic that runs throughout our society — art makes the whole beastly materialism of life and society bearable. In actual fact what makes the beastly world so bearable is precisely the chance to belong to the elite that can lecture at an institution that expresses this ideology where it is economically bearable to live in the beastly world . . . i.e. the ethic arises out of and reinforces the social situation.(10)

The revolutionary alternative is not, however, to be seen in the work of Basil Bernstein, as suggested by Hoare (though this may have seemed more likely in 1967) but in the type of work being done today by Chris Searle(11) and Ken Worpole.(12)

References

1   The Bullock Report A Language for Life, HMSO 1975.
2   Peter Doughty, 'What remains to do', in *English in Education* Vol. 2. No. 3 Autumn 1968.
    Fred Flower, 'English in Further Education', in *English in Education* Vol. 4 No. 1 Spring 1970.
    D.F. Bratchell, 'Non-Specialist English Studies in Higher Education, in *English in Education*, Vol. 5, No. 1 Spring 1971.
3   Fred Inglis, 'How to do things with words', in *English in Education*, Vo. 5 No. 2 Summer 1971.
4   F.R. Leavis, *The Great Tradition*, Chatto & Windus 1948.
5   Georg Lukacs, *Writer & Critic*, Merlin Press 1970.
6   P. McGeeney, 'Bernstein of Compensatory Education', in *English in Education*, Vol. 4, No. 3 Autumn 1970.

7   E.P. Clark, 'Language and Politics in Education', in *English in Education*, Vol. 5 No. 2 Summer 1971.

8   D.F. Mahon, 'Language Development in Infants', in *English in Education*, Vol. 4 No. 3 Autumn 1970.

9   T. Hale, 'Teaching Poetry Through Rock Music', in *English in Education*, Vol. 5 No. 1 Spring 1971.

10   Michael Rosen, *Doing Eng. Lit., in ed.* Trevor Pateman — Counter Course. Penguin 1972.

11   Chris Searle, *Classrooms of Resistance*, Writers and Readers Publishing Cooperative 1975.

12   Ken Worpole, *Activities of Centerprise*, 136-138 Kingsland High St., London E8 2NS.

The History and Politics of Literacy
Martin Hoyles

The Origins and Development of Writing(1)

The cave-paintings at Lascaux seem a far cry from the printing on this page; but just as visual symbolism may have been the precursor of speech,(2) primitive drawings contain the seeds of writings. Crucially the picture, like the word, is an abstraction — it refers to something absent. Paintings of deer being hunted or a rain ceremony are celebrations of a past (or future) event; either a record of what's gone or an attempt to influence the future through magic. It is from such images that our writing system stems: 'At the basis of all writings stands the picture — geometric designs do not represent abstract forms but are the result of a schematic development from real pictures.'(3)

Pictures can also communicate a message, and this function seems closer to that of writing. An Indian rock drawing on a mountain trail in New Mexico shows an upright goat and a fallen horse, indicating a precipitous trail which a mountain goat could climb but where a horse would tumble down. This kind of image, however, leads not to writing but to sign language, like the highway code or certain conventions in silent films and comic strips — which can easily be understood internationally because they do not rely directly on spoken language.

A more direct precursor of written language is the picture used for identifying or mnemonic purposes, based on the need for recording rather than sending messages. Red-Cloud's Census in 1884 contained drawings to indicate the names of people (like heraldic signs in the middle ages; or the symbols of crafts, e.g. key=locksmith, pair of glasses=optician). Names and the concomitant idea of property are very significant in the development of writing: 'The seal, as a mark of ownership, is the parent of writing and printing.'(4)

Through pictorial means, history can be recorded before the development of a writing system. The Dakota Winter Counts were a way of remembering the years by assigning to each a sign representing the most significant event of the year. On a more abstract level the Peruvian Incas could record events by means of *quipu* writing, a series of strings and knots meaning different things according to their length and colour. Similar use of objects as mnemonic devices is made by West African singers who keep a net full of pipes, feathers, skins, birdheads, bones, etc., each one recalling a certain song in their repertoire.

The first great breakthrough in the invention of writing, as we know it, was the development of word-signs that recur consistently as standardised symbols. So instead of drawing a picture of a man killing a stag, you could use three symbols in sequence — MAN, SPEAR, STAG. Sumerian clay tablets found in southern Mesopotamia (now Iraq) show that this form of writing was in existence some 5,000 years ago.

Word-signs developed from being simple, primary symbols (e.g. a circle indicating the sun) to having associative meanings where the circle could also mean white or day. But the single most important step in the history of writing, the phonetic transfer, occurred when the circle could also stand for a boy: i.e. *SON*. Or a picture of an arrow could mean either an arrow or life because the word *ti* meant both. Phonetization arose from the need to express words and sounds which could not be adequately indicated by pictures. Its principle consists in associating words which are difficult to express in writing with signs which resemble these words in sound and are easy to draw: e.g. drawing an eye and a saw to mean 'I saw' (rebus writing).

In Yoruba you can strike up a relationship by means of cowrie shells, based on the same phonetic principle. Six cowrie shells mean 'attracted' (I love you) because the word *efa* means both six and attractive. *Eyo* means eight and also agreed, so eight cowrie shells mean 'agreed' (I love you too)!

From word-signs the final major development was the alphabet, by way of the syllabary. The syllabary, with a sign for each syllable, was in evidence in Crete around 1600 B.C. The alphabet developed between Egypt and Mesopotamia, in what is now Syria and Palestine around 1400 B.C., but it contained no vowels. The Greeks first made regular use of vowels in their alphabet (which was originally brought to them by the Phoenicians about the ninth century B.C.). Greek letters were derived from names for whole words: e.g. aleph − ox, beth − house, gimel − camel, deleth − door, (alpha, beta, gamma, delta). Finally our own alphabet − the Roman one − developed from the Greek via the Etruscan.

So much for the technical invention of writing; but what of the reasons for it? Clearly, one is that of basic economic need, as R.L. Gregory points out in his chapter on the history of writing:

> Thought is primarily concerned with the properties and potentialities of objects, for it is these that are important for survival. Above all, thought is concerned with predicting the immediate future, and if necessary changing it to avoid disaster or gain reward. It is interesting that the content and subject-matter of the early languages is not philosophy or abstract speculation, but lists of possessions, accounts of victories in war and elaborate funeral observances for the dead (with the hope of continuing life's pleasures).(5)

Just as nomadic hunters at the end of the ice age had a knowledge of astronomy to forecast the seasons and to migrate to new hunting grounds, so the settled community life of the Neolithic period led to the idea of proprietorship − which in turn led to tribute-payment and accountancy, and hence the need for records of enumeration:

> Sumerian writing owes its origin to needs arising from public economy and administration. With the rise in productivity of the country resulting from state-controlled canalization and irrigation systems, the accumulated agricultural surplus made its way to the depots and granaries of the cities, necessitating keeping accounts of goods coming to the cities, as well as of manufactured products leaving the cities for the country.(6)

We tend to think of literacy in the middle ages as being the preserve of the church and legal profession, but it was just as important commercially for merchants and ship pilots. The high-rate of literacy in Venice came about because it was needed for navigation. Even soldiers needed to be literate to read gun manuals. The high rate of literacy in Scotland can partly be explained by reference to the Clarendon Code which deprived English non-conformists of the right to hold public office till 1824 and the right of university residence till 1870.(7)

Cultural exchange seems to have been important in the development of writing. This occurred through trade and conquest. The Middle East was a great cultural melting-pot. Here, around 1000 B.C., the Babylonian, Assyrian, Minoan, Hittite and Egyptian cultures declined, while the Israelites, Phoenicians, Aramaeans and Greeks rose to take their place. Perhaps this explains why the same phonetic development in writing did not occur in China or in South America (Mayan) which were more isolated.

The same sort of cultural diffusion is seen as crucial in the development of symbolization in mathematics:

> Out of the letter writing which followed the phonetic pictures of the words, how could the concept symbols of mathematics spring up? . . . In Egypt, with its historical continuity, this step did not take place. In Babylon, where two entirely different cultures, the Sumerian and the Akkadian (with languages of basically distinct grammatical types) are superimposed, the path for such a formal development was cleared . . . Through

the contact of these distinct languages there arose the possibility of writing a word either by syllables or by ideograms. In the Akkadian texts both modes of writing are arbitrarily used in turn; thereby arose the possibility of writing the mathematical concepts (quantities and operations) ideographically and of attaining a language of formulae, while the remaining text is written in syllables.(8)

Religious and political crusades helped the spread of writing. During the growth of Islam the Arabic alphabet was adopted in all lands from Spain to Indonesia; and later the Jews made available to Europe the fruits of Greek learning through Arabic translations current in the Moslem world. The Jewish community has always been literate — on the male side! — because of the obligation to bring up a boy in the works of Mosaic Law.

The materials used obviously influence the form of writing. For example cuneiform developed its wedge-shape because it was written on clay or wood. The origin of the word to write means to carve, incise, or paint. The invention of paper (in China in 105 A.D.) led to different styles of writing; while the general artistic style of a period can influence the style of writing. For instance, the roundness of Carolingian hand-writing corresponds to Romanesque architecture, and the angular Gothic script to Gothic architecture.

Writing — But for Whom?

Once a system of writing is invented, people have to be initiated into its conventions; and historically these people have been the select few: 'In my eyes authors, journalists, and artists stood for a world which was more attractive than any other, one open only to the elect.'(9) They have nearly always held political power — or they have been used by those with power. Kings could be illiterate, like William the Conqueror, but they paid clerks to read and write for them. In Tahiti the nobles were responsible for the calendar; in New Zealand the priests; in China the literati formed a formidable group of administrators. Those without the skills of literacy often looked upon them as having magical powers — hence the myth of the gods inventing writing.

When each book was unique, this reverence for books was more understandable; but even since the coming of print, books still retain an aura of magic about them. Perhaps now it is because of their permanence and seeming authority: 'I had always worshipped authors. I used to kiss their pictures on the backs of books when I finished reading. I regarded anything printed as a holy relic and authors as creatures of superhuman knowledge and wit.'(10)

But this all depends on your experience of literacy and on your point of view. It also depends on what books are available. For Simone de Beauvoir, books were the window on the world: 'When I was a child and an adolescent, reading was not only my favourite pastime, but also the key that opened the world to me. It foretold my future: I identified myself with the heroines of novels, and through them I caught glimpses of what my life would be. In the unhappy phases of my youth it preserved me from loneliness; later it broadened my knowledge, increased my experience and helped me to a better understanding of my state as a human being and of the meaning of my work as a writer.'(11) Whereas for the author of an article in the Socialist Standard of 1905, books masked the truth: 'As to the school books used, history and science, in fact all subjects more or less, are interpreted with a view to convincing the prospective toilers of the necessity for the existence of competition, class distinction and the struggle for a paltry sustenance for ever and ever.'(12)

Illiteracy can be seen as a way of escaping an oppressive ideology,(13) as Clara Zetkin argued with Lenin, though she seems to have neglected to consider other ways in which 'bourgeois ideas and conceptions' can be transmitted:

> 'While in Moscow today ten thousand — and tomorrow another ten thousand — are charmed by brilliant theatrical performances, millions are crying out to learn the art of spelling, of writing their names, of counting, are crying for culture, are anxious to learn, for they are beginning to understand that the universe is ruled by natural laws, and not by the 'Heavenly Father', and his witches and wizards.'
>
> 'Don't complain so bitterly of the illiteracy, Comrade Lenin,' I interjected. 'To a certain extent it really helped forward the revolution. It prevented the mind of the workers and peasants from being stopped up and corrupted with bourgeois ideas and conceptions. Your propaganda and agitation is falling on virgin soil. It is easier to sow and to reap where you have not first of all to uproot a whole forest.'
>
> 'Illiteracy was compatible with the struggle for the seizure of power, with the necessity to destroy the old State apparatus . . . Illiteracy is incompatible with the tasks of construction.'(14)

Trotsky, however, tells of the desperate attempt by Marxist workers in Russia to get hold of socialist texts:

> Abandoned by their former leaders, the workers' circles continued to seek their roads independently. They read much and searched out in old and new magazines articles about the life of West European workers, trying to see whether these were applicable to themselves. One of the first Marxist workers, Shelgunov, recalls that in 1887-8, that is, the most terrible times, 'workers' circles were growing more and more . . .
> Progressive workers. . . were looking for books and buying them from second-hand dealers'. These books had, undoubtedly come into the hands of second-hand dealers from disenchanted members of the intelligentsia. Rare-book dealers charged forty to fifty roubles for a volume of 'Das Kapital'. Still, Petersburg workers managed to get hold of that precious book. 'I myself', writes Shelgunov, 'had to tear up 'Das Kapital' into parts into chapters, so that it would be read simultaneously in three or four circles.'(15)

With the development of modern means of communication, writing seems not so crucial as a means of acquiring or transmitting knowledge and values. But technological media contain the same ambiguities and contradictions. Television was withheld in South Africa for fear of arousing black envy of white living-standards. While in this country, television conveys a dominant ideology (for instance, always against strikes) under the guise of BBC objectivity.

Writing began in the first big urban centres as response to commercial and military need. Similarly, print developed in the growing towns marking the rise of the bourgeoisie. But print was part of a whole new way of looking at writing: its use and value, new authors and new readers — Reformation and Renaissance.

Script	Print
Feudal	Bourgeois
International	National
Latin	National Language
Varied Orthography	Accuracy
Changeable Texts	Permanence and Authority
Reading Aloud	Private Silent Reading
Authorship Unimportant	Authorship and Copyright
Copying Approved	Idea of Plagiarism
Books Bequeathed in Wills	Books Commonplace
Illiteracy	Middle-class Literacy

These two lists show in a broad way the relationship between changes in society and changes in communication. Looking at them, it becomes clear that our present system of communication is not inevitable. For example, reading does not need to be a private affair, for in the middle ages reading aloud was common. Similarly, copyright has been abolished in Cuba, 'because it is felt that a work of art should not be subjected to commercial mechanisms which, for that matter, are not operative in our country; because it is deemed that the product of man's intellect is the property and heritage of all mankind and, finally, because for a creator in a society like ours, the act of creation and the possibility of giving the thing created to the people is incentive enough.'(16)

The most crucial area of all, now as in the past, is that

of control. Who controls the media of communication? As Hans Magnus Enzensberger argues, it's no use complaining about manipulation per se because every use of the media presupposes manipulation:

> All technical manipulations are potentially dangerous; the manipulation of the media cannot be countered, however, by old or new forms of censorship, but only by direct social control, that is to say, by the mass of the people, who will have become productive. To this end, the elimination of capitalistic property relationships is a necessary, but by no means sufficient condition. There have been no historical examples up until now of the mass self-regualting learning process which is made possible by the electronic media. The Communists' fear of releasing this potential, of the mobilising capabilities of the media, of the interaction of free producers, is one of the main reasons why even in the socialist countries, the old bourgeois culture, greatly disguised and distorted but structually intact, continues to hold sway.(17)

This fear of the mobilising capabilities of the media has often been in evidence in connection with the written word. Cortez destroyed the written treasures of the Aztecs; the Inquisition suppressed books; the Nazis burnt them. (Similarly with technological media: as witness the suppression of Douglas Lowndes' Viewpoint series of School broadcasts on Thames Television, which questioned the whole ideological framework of the media.) The only way to overcome this suppression, as Enzensberger says, is through direct social control of the media by the mass of the people.

The Politics of Literacy: Repression or Liberation?

What then are we doing when we teach children to read and write? We have taken this for granted for so long that it seems strange to question it. But is it a liberating or a repressive activity? Neil Postman writes: 'If you cannot read, you cannot be an obedient citizen. An important function of the teaching of reading is to make students accessible to political and historical myth.'(18) And Enzensberger argues that, 'Intimidation through the written word has remained a widespread and class-specific phenomenon even in advanced industrial societies.'(19)

So what is the point of teaching pupils to read and write? Would it not be better to ignore these activities altogether and concentrate on oral methods of education? This conclusion is absurd, for the important thing to do is to examine the context in which children read and write and see how that context can be changed. This is the purpose of studying literacy from a historical and social perspective.

The introduction of writing made illiterates inevitable — especially as in Chinese you had to learn at least 3,000 characters (out of 50,000) to be reasonably literate. In China only a small and specially trained professional group partook of literary culture. Max Weber shows what power these literati wielded over the centuries.(20) A literary education was the yardstick of social prestige — it was not hereditary or exclusive, but controlled by a system of examinations. The ancient scriptures were considered holders of a magical charisma. Written symbols were thought to be superior to the spoken word and the literary product was addressed more to the eyes than the ears.

The writing system (especially when non-phonetic) acted as a strong conservative force to maintain the power of the literate elite. For Marx this was one of the first divisions of labour; and an ancient Egyptian confirms it: 'Put writing in your heart that you may protect yourself from hard labour of any kind. The scribe is released from manual tasks; it is he who commands.'(21)

The crucial phonetic change, already referred to, has been called a transition from a theocratic script to a democratic script, because of the closer connection between the alphabet and speech. (Compare, however, El Lissitsky's point that 'the hieroglyphic book is international, the alphabetical book is national.'(22) Similarly, the silent movies were international whereas the coming of sound brought problems of dubbing and sub-titling.) Nevertheless, far from becoming a mass medium of communication, writing retained its religious and elitist character. Hebrew culture continued to be transmitted orally long after the Old Testament had begun to be written down: 'The written book is not intended for practical use at all. It is a divine instrument, placed in the temple 'by the side of the ark of the covenant that it may be there for a witness' and remains there as a holy relic . . Writing was practised, if at all, only as an additional support for the memory.'(23)

According to Goody and Watt 'it was in the sixth and fifth centuries B.C. in the city states of Greece and Ionia that there first arose a society which as a whole could justly be characterised as literate.' They give as evidence that 'a majority of the free citizens could apparently read the laws, and take an active part in elections and legislation'; but as this excluded women and slaves, it was clearly not a majority of the people.(24)

As we have seen, the skill of reading and writing has rested in the hands of elites who have held considerable power and have used their literacy to keep illiterate people in awe. Also the literati themselves have been greatly influenced by the weight and tradition of the ancient texts. As has been said, these texts were often venerated in themselves apart from the content; they were sacred objects and kept in special places. They were either originals or copies made by hand. So their possession was a privilege reserved for only a few. Books were not available for the mass of the people.

Revolutionising the Bourgeois Tradition

All this changed fundamentally with the invention of printing at the end of the fifteenth century. Walter Benjamin (although writing primarily about photography and the cinema) refers to the theoretical significance of this shift to mechanical production:

> The technique of reproduction detaches the reproduced object from the domain of tradition. By making many reproductions it substitutes a plurality of copies for a unique existence. And in permitting the reproduction to meet the beholder or listener in his own particular situation, it reactivates the object reproduced. These two processes lead to a tremendous shattering of tradition.(25)

The shattering of tradition connected with the printed word was, of course, the Reformation. Postman argues that the invention of printing generated cataclysmic changes: the Reformation and Capitalism — as well as the novel and essay, exams and scientific methodology(26) (though it would seem more reasonable to see the Reformation and birth of Capitalism as bringing about the printed word.) What is important, however, is the interaction between social and technical change; and particularly important the fact that the written word was now being used to intimidate those in power, as well as the other way round.

In sixteenth century England, for example, literature was used by both sides in the struggle between Catholics and Protestants. The Catholic miracle and morality plays were systematically banned and Protestant propaganda plays were written to be performed instead. In 1538 censorship of books in English was introduced. An Act of 1543 forbade the reading of any English Bible by artificers, journeymen, serving-men under the rank of yeoman, husbandmen, labourers, and all women other than those of noble or gentle rank.

The rising bourgeoisie used the written word to help

them effect their revolution and gain power. Milton wrote for Cromwell. The Royal Society in the seventeenth century was given the taks of creating a rational prose style to meet the needs of scientific research.

But once in power, the bourgeoisie changes its attitude to writing — it becomes a method of control rather than rebellion. The American Declaration of Independence proved an embarrassment once the national bourgeoisie achieved power. The study of literature becomes one way of civilising the children of the middle-classes and inculcating the dominant culture. The poor too must learn to read the bible for moral reasons — although writing was thought a bit dangerous by some people in the nineteenth century.(27) Instead, class struggle is now considered irrelevant by the bourgeoisie and literary culture is placed above class interest. So Matthew Arnold once wrote, 'Culture seeks to do away with classes'; and Northrop Frye today, 'The ethical purpose of a liberal education is to make one capable of conceiving society as free, classless, and urbane.'

Certain forms and styles of writing were developed appropriate to bourgeois values, and these are still believed to represent high culture. In literature, the novel is the height of this development — written by one individual to be read in private by another individual. It is interesting that although the nineteenth century Romantic movement was in part a reaction against the industrial revolution; it was still trapped within this individualistic isolation. Louis Kampf writes about the narcissistic self obsession of modern literature and the tragic isolation of the individual, which leads to a feeling of pessimism and helplessness. He points out that 'the notion of culture as high culture — with its values of complexity, irony and tragic acceptance — implies the necessity of an elite of technocrat-critics.'(28) Similarly, Ellen Cantarow makes the point that bourgeois literature celebrates individual exploits and sees the perfecting of the individual as the best social goal.(29) Repercussions of this ideal are apparent in educational circles as professional individualism, competition, mutual distrust and isolation. So pupils are taught to compete with each other, especially when they take exams; and right the way to the top of our educational ladder, achievement must be individual. Higher education's career structure is shaped like a pyramid. Individual Ph.D. research and publication is the way to the top.

Likewise in history — individual aggression dominates a topsy-turvy world picture. The masses are seen as the passive and grateful recipients of the discoveries of certain heroic individuals — as illustrated by Bertolt Brecht's poem, 'A Worker Questions History':

> Young Alexander conquered India.
> On his own?
> Caesar beat the Gauls.
> Didn't he at least have a cook with him?
> Philip of Spain wept when his fleet
> Was destroyed. Did no one else weep?(30)

All this has an effect on the dominated culture — in Marx's terms as false consciousness, in Paulo Freire's as the dominators living within the dominated,(31) or in Frantz Fanon's as Black Skin, White Masks.(32) This is what leads Kampf to say: 'No one had ever told us that initiating the 'underprivileged' to the cultural treasures of the west could be a form of oppression — more insidiously, a weapon in the hands of those who rule.' And Martha Vicinus, in her analysis of nineteenth century British Working Class Poetry, refers to the increased acceptance of middle class values and customs and the separation of poetry from life.(33) This last aspect is clearly meant to give the impression that literature is timeless and 'above the petty details of any one person's daily living.'(34) Also it is an attempt to destroy any revolutionary potential in literature.

Nevertheless this ideological colonialism is by no

means uncontested. There are other cultures and other forms of the written word which challenge the dominant culture. Lenin in *What is to be done* (1902) emphasised the importance of the party newspaper; and the threat of revolutionary newspapers was clearly seen in nineteenth century England when heavy taxation of newspapers and a series of prosecutions were both imposed with the aim of killing the whole radical press. The widespread nature of the 'corresponding societies' also illustrates the importance of the written word in the Chartist movement and the growth of the Labour movement.(35)

In the twentieth century, communist revolutions have shown the galvanising effect of the written word, in a collective rather than a private form. In China, newspapers were read to groups of workers and peasants; editorials and articles were copied on to tens of thousands of wall-boards; and radio stations read them over the air. Similarly, Lissitsky tells us about the colossal labour of propaganda and enlightenment undertaken during the Russian Revolution: 'We ripped up the traditional book into single pages, magnified these a hundred times, printed them in colour and stuck them up as posters in the streets.'(36)

Some people have believed that when literacy became universal, it would bring about freedom and equality for all. J.S. Mill refers to his father's faith in this idea:

> So complete was my father's reliance on the influence of reason over the minds of mankind, whenever it is allowed to reach them, that he felt as if all would be gained if the whole population were taught to read, if all sorts of opinions were allowed to be addressed to them by word and in writing, and if, by means of the suffrage they could nominate a legislature to give effect to the opinions they adopted.

In this country we have majority — if not universal — literacy. According to Raymond Williams, there was a majority Sunday newspaper public in 1910, a majority daily newspaper public by 1918, and a majority book-reading public by the 1950s.(37) Yet this has not brought about any basic change in the power structure of our society.

Literacy is a two-edged sword. It can be repressive or liberating: 'Literature and literary practice . . . are weapons in maintaining or transforming the received order of social relations.' Kampf and Lauter go on to acknowledge that 'in our culture the reading of literature is pacifying, it often separates people from action instead of leading them into it.' But they add, 'This is by no means necessary.'(38)

Enzensberger comes down on the side of those who consider the book repressive. He acknowledges the revolutionary and progressive role of the printed book for the bourgeoisie, but sees its structure now as authoritarian compared with the oral word: 'While people learn to speak very early, and mostly in psychologically favourable conditions, learning to write forms an important part of authoritarian socialization by the school.' Written language encourages the repression of opposition and the smoothing out of contradictions: 'Structurally, the printed book is a medium that operates as a monologue isolating producer and reader.' According to Enzensberger 'these alienating factors cannot be eradicated from written literature.'(39)

Freire, on the other hand, emphasises the liberating powers of literacy, especially in Latin America. Reading and writing are a form of objectification which gives people the means of transforming reality: 'The dominated can eject the dominators only by getting distance from them and objectifying them.' (cf. the idea of writing enabling the change to be made from myth to history.) Peasants had no need to read and write when they simply did as they were told; now they need to in order to organise their work: 'As they learn to read peasants discover that they are creators of culture.' Brecht also sees the book as a weapon for liberation:

You who are starving, grab hold of the book: it's a weapon.
You must take over the leadership. (40)

Much depends on motive, context and method. Why are people being taught to read and write? Is it to control them — or free them? And how much control does the learner have over the process? Freire talks about finding the peasants' key concepts first before teaching them by using these concepts. But compare this with the use of a set text-book! Similarly, in China lessons are in the form of folk and work songs and political education comes first to explain why literacy is so important. Literacy is needed for organising the commune.(41) Yet, the destruction of coherence may be caused by pushing reading into context-less space, as Wayne O'Neil describes it: 'Reading is taught as if it were another language, another world, not as if it were a highly abstract representation of the language that the child has tacit knowledge of. Intuitive connections are erased. And so is knowledge.'

Most of the time we don't question the purpose of literacy. In school its function so often seems simply one of social control. If it is to be liberating, the problem is how to *change* the context. Modern English teaching is meant to have achieved some sort of a breakthrough in this respect; but the pupils may well think creative writing is simply a more demanding form of imposed drudgery than copying out of a book — and anyway it's a pin-prick compared to the teacher's normal daily routine and the pupils' total educational experience. The problem is how to revolutionize the *total* context.(42)

References

1   David Diringer, *Writing,* Thames and Hudson 1962.
     H.J. Chaytor, *From Script to Print,* C.U.P. 1945.
     Carlo M. Cipolla, *Literacy and Development in the West,* Penguin 1969.

2   Susanne K. Langer, *Philosophical Sketches*, John Hopkins Press 1962.
3   I.J. Gelb, *A Study of Writing*, Chicago 1952
4   L. Hogben, *From Cave Painting to Comic Strip*, Max Parrish 1949.
5   R.L. Gregory, *The Intelligent Eye*, Weidenfeld and Nicholson 1970.
6   I.J. Gelb, op.cit.
7   L. Hogben, op.cit.
8   Raymond L. Wilder, *Evolution of Mathematical Concepts*, Transworld 1974.
9   Leon Trotsky,*My Life*, Penguin 1975.
10 E. Jong, *Fear of Flying*, Panther 1974.
11 Simone de Beauvoir, *All Said and Done*, Warner 1975.
12 The Socialist Standard, January 7, 1905.
13 Neil Postman, 'The Politics of Reading', in ed. Nell Keddie, *Tinker, Tailor . . .*, Penguin 1973.
14 Clara Zetkin, *Reminiscences of Lenin*, Modern Books 1929
15 Leon Trotsky, *The Young Lenin*, Penguin 1974.
16 Lisandro Otero, *Cultural Policy in Cuba*, Unesco Paris 1972.
17 Hans Magnus Enzensberger, 'Constituents of a Theory of the Media,' *New Left Review*, No. 64 1970.
18 Neil Postman, op.cit.
19 Hans Magnus Enzensberger, op.cit.
20 Max Weber, 'The Chinese Literati', in From Max Weber: *Essays in Sociology*, O.U.P. 1946.
21 J. Goody & I. Watt, 'The Consequences of Literacy', in ed. Pier Paolo Giglioli, *Language and Social Context*, Penguin 1972.
22 El Lissitsky, 'The Future of the Book', *New Left Review No. 41*.
23 J Goody & I. Watt, op. cit.
24 Ibid.
25 Walter Benjamin, 'The World of Art in the Age of Mechanical Reproduction', in *Illuminations*, Jonathan Cape 1970.
26 Neil Postman, op.cit.
27 Raymond Williams, *The Long Revolution*, Penguin 1965.
28 Louis Kampf, 'The Trouble with Literature', *Change*, May 1970.
29 Ellen Cantarow, 'The Radicalisation of a Teacher of Literature', *Change*, May 1972.
30 Bertolt Brecht, *Gedichte*, Reclam 1958.
31 Paulo Freire, 'The Adult Literacy Process as Cultural Action for Freedom', *Harvard Educational Review*, Vol.40 No.2 1970.

32 Frantz Fanon, *Black Skins, White Masks,* MacGibbon & Kee 1968.

33 Martha Vicinus, 'Nineteenth Century British Working Class Poetry', in ed.
   Louis Kampf & Paul Lauter, *The Politics of Literature,* Vintage Books 1973.

34 Ellen Cantarow, op.cit.

35 E.P. Thompson, *The Making of the English Working Class,* Penguin 1970.

36 El Lissitsky, op.cit.

37 Raymond Williams, op.cit.

38 Louis Kampf & Paul Lauter, op.cit.

39 Hans Magnus Enzensberger, op.cit.

40 Bertolt Brecht, op.cit.

41 R.F. Price, *Education in Communist China,* Routledge 1970.

42 This issue is taken up again in the last section of the book.

Education: Programmes and People
Quintin Hoare

British education is from a rational point of view grotesque, from a moral one intolerable, and from a human one tragic. Few would deny its stark inadequacy. Predictably, the Labour Party has at no time offered a global challenge to the present system. It has at most stood for its expansion and the elimination of some of its most flagrantly undemocratic features. It has never seriously threatened the most structurally important of these: the continued existence of the public schools, and sexual discrimination against girls in every type of school. Above all, it has never attacked the vital centre of the system, the curriculum, the *content* of what is taught.

However, a reorganization of secondary education is at the moment in progress, a reorganization which is largely to the credit of the Labour Party.

Although it represents a minimal reform, and timidly executed at that, it does unfreeze the existing situation and put a question mark over the whole system, just as the various governmental reports have done. Comprehensive education as it is at present conceived is little more than a rationalization of the *status quo*. But the change to comprehensive education involves a major political conflict and educational debate, which offer real possibilities for moving beyond the conventional interpretations of the comprehensive idea. In this situation, socialists should be trying to clarify the terms of educational discussion, and to escalate the political struggle for comprehensive education so that it invests an ever-increasing area of the entire educational nexus: curriculum, teaching methods, textbooks, school organization, organization of the teaching profession.

A period of educational reform is certainly imminent, whichever party is in power during the years to come; the demands of the economy cannot be gainsaid much longer. It is essential, then, that the left should be prepared and able to counterpose to the mere insistence on greater *investment* in education,(1) demands which affect the whole character of the educational process: demands concerning the content of what is taught, and the purpose of education itself.

There is, at present, wide-spread opposition to the existing system, from parents, from teachers, and not least from children. This opposition has taken various forms, each of which contains its moment of truth. Thus a key task for socialists today is to analyse the nature and historical development of British education in all its aspects, and to criticize the main theoretical traditions which have accompanied this development. A socialist theory of education, whose aim must be to confront the educational system as a whole, can only be built on this basis. This article is intended to do no more than indicate some of the initial problems which would be posed by such an attempt.

The educational process cannot be reduced to any single function. It is at the same time:

1 A process of *socialization*, of internalization of dominant social *norms* and *values*. This process can be considered from the viewpoint of the whole society, or from that of the developing individual personality.

2 A process of *acculturation* of the rising generation, in which it inherits a common repertory of *ideas* and *symbols* (of which the most important aspect is literacy).

3 A system of *vocational training*, which transmits specific skills for use in later life.

4 The process by which in any society *intellectuals* and *culture* are formed.

These functions of education may overlap at points, but they are distinct; each is present in some degree in any educational system. It follows that education is an absolutely distinctive social phenomenon in two ways. Social-democracy has always tended to consider education as a social service similar in kind to housing or medicine; in other words, as a 'good' which should be shared more equally, and which can be increased in a purely quantitative way. This view, however, overlooks the very special ambiguity of education. For on the one hand, it represents a vital human *need* — common to all societies and all people in some form, and as basic as subsistence or shelter. On the other hand, it is a fundamental component of the power structure in any society —the means whereby assent is secured to the values and privileges of the dominant class. Education, in fact, is the point at which vital needs and power structure *immediately intersect.* It is thus never neutral or 'innocent', as the other social services can sometimes be. Houses are houses, and the more of them the better; but education is never just 'education' — it is the assimilation of a social order.

The second distinctive aspect of education is that it is a self-perpetuating system, with a feedback mechanism. For the consciousness and outlook of the teachers condition the developing consciousness of the pupils who will themselves provide the next generation of teachers, and so on. The problem for socialists is then to break this circle, and to do so clearly involves not merely thinking in a socialist perspective about education, but also thinking about educating socialists — for the two tasks ultimately converge.

Returning to the model suggested above, the various functions of education can be differentiated not merely analytically, but historically as well. Different schools have at different times emphasized different educational functions. Medieval schools in Britain were principally vocational schools, training priests in Latin and singing. But they also inculcated Christian culture and values, and the priests who emerged from them were in fact the intellectuals of feudal society. The early universities were based on vocational faculties—law, medicine, theology—but they developed the conception of 'liberal education'.(3)

The early public schools from their foundation were enabled by their independence from church or monastery to recruit nationally, thus laying the basis for their later development as the schools of the dominant class. But their major period of expansion during the last century represented the fusion of the most dynamic elements of the industrial bourgeoisie with the governing class, based on the very high degree of ideological integration necessary to dominate the immense social changes consequent on industrialization and the rise of the working class. The principal function of these schools was clearly a socializing one. They aimed to develop the *general* capacity and confidence to govern, and their central emphasis was on the development of *character* (as opposed to knowledge or skills).

The non-conformist Dissenting Academics of the 18th century, in which the modern curriculum took shape, provided an indispensable acculturation for sections of the rising middle classes in the face of a complete failure on the part of the traditional institutions to adapt to a changing economy and an expanding culture. To some extent this function subsists in the modern grammar schools, although the logic of their position now forces them to view education principally in an instrumental way, as the means by which they can compete with the public schools in terms of the life-chances of the pupils. Where the public school stresses 'character', the grammar school must stress 'intelligence'.

The development of state secondary education on the other hand was an explicit response to the demands of the economy, and the three-tier structure introduced by the Taunton Commission in 1867 shows this quite plainly: the three tiers were to correspond to ranks in later life. The modern tripartite system echoes those divisions, and within it the bottom tier—secondary modern education— must be considered as primarily concerned with the transmission of specific, predominantly manual, skills.

Thus the full weight of the hierarchic and anti-democratic character of British education can only be appreciated when its structure is related to the whole fabric of British society, and when its function as a basic component of the power structure is considered. It is in this context that the question of destroying the public schools should be seen. That they provide privileged roads to the top is important, but secondary. The primary reason why the private sector must be liquidated is that it is the key element in the formation and continued pre-eminence of the existing hegemonic class, that it has functioned and still functions as a model for the entire public system, which is infected by its curricula, its values, its organizational forms and its style. The morning prayers and the prize-giving, the prefect-system and the sports, the competition and the sex-segregation and the compulsory teaching of religion,(4) which are to be found throughout the schools of Britain not excepting the comprehensives—all these are a miserable calque on the public school model. The dangers implicit in the slogan of 'integration' of the private sector into the public system hardly need emphasizing.

During the last 90 years there has been a massive if belated expansion of public education in Britain. Primary education was extended to all children in 1876-80, and secondary education to the age of 15 in 1944. There have been two main pressures behind this expansion: on the one hand the demands of the working-class for education. But in practice, it has been the demands of the economy which have *structured* the expansion. Thus the polarities of British education can be seen as on the one hand hierarchy and restriction, and on the other vocationalism. Their co-existence defines the present system. The vocational conception of education dominates the secondary modern school, the teaching of science in every kind of school, and the technical schools; its increasing prevalence in grammar schools and universities can also be observed, and is the rationale behind the uniquely early school specialization in this country.

The vocational character of the education system is further emphasized by the increasing participation of industry in 'vocational guidance' during the final years of school, and the freedom given to industry to recruit within the schools. No-one who has seen the main hall of a comprehensive turned into a recruiting agency for industry towards the end of a school year will be unaware of the main function of the school.

Perhaps most important of all, the segregation of girls and boys into separate schools, and the differential education which they receive even in such coeducational schools as there are (there is little differentiation in the first years of primary education, but it is already unmistakable by the age of eight or nine, and rises steadily to reach a peak in the last year of compulsory education) have a clearly vocational character.(6) This is true both in the simple sense that an increasingly different curriculum conditions future choice of job, and directs girls into 'women's' jobs, but more important still in the sense that segregation reinforces the ideology of women's role as distinct from that of men, and conditions them to accept as theirs the unpaid labour of domestic work and child-rearing. Of course, indoctrination of women begins at home, in a literal sense, but the point is that the education system instead of combating this compounds it.

To recapitulate briefly, we have an education dominated at the top by the values and models of the private sector; and an education whose massive growth from below during the last century has been shaped almost entirely by simple laws of supply and demand. What, meanwhile, has been the evolution of educational thought in the modern period? Educational expansion in this century has not been accompanied by any fundamental reformulation of educational aims, or by any flowering of educational theory. It is, however, possible to isolate four main schools of educational thought, each of which contains a partial validity; it is only by criticizing them that a socialist alternative can be concretely posed. They can be characterized as, respectively, the conservatives, the rationalizers, the romantics and the democrats.

The Conservative Position

The conservative position—extremely strong among university and grammar school teachers—represents the rearguard action of elite education, of the classical curriculum, and of the intellectuals who are subordinate to it.(7) Sometimes this can take the form simply of crude resistance to change, as in Amis' *More will be worse.* Sometimes it rests on a more conscious and elaborated conservative ideology such as that of Eliot, Oakeshott, Leavis or Bantock,(8) or on an articulated pseudo-scientific view of human intelligence such as that of Burt.(9) Its concern for 'high culture' might be seen as partially defensible for all its undemocratic implications, were its programme not so manifestly and pathetically a defence of the *status quo,* as a few quotations from Bantock will show: 'My 'plan', then, has none of the heroic proportions of the others. It involves achievement by means of 'small adjustments and re-adjustments which can be continually improved upon' . . . Existing good schools would remain untouched . . . The most that can be expected is a reasonable degree of mobility—and this, at least, has been achieved.'(10) When it comes down to actual prescriptions, and above all to the curriculum, 'concern for high culture' is revealed as Oakeshottian defence of the existing system, with a dash of Popperian piecemeal tinkering and more domestic education for those girls and more manual education for those boys who are 'less able'.

The survival of this school of thought, although it is making its stand in defence of the grammar school and against university expansion, is in fact made possible principally by the survival of the private sector of education and of a similarly aristocratic conception of education in Oxford and Cambridge, and their deeply hierarchical influence on the whole educational system. The extent to which provincial universities are subordinate to the models and values of Oxford and Cambridge hardly needs stressing, nor the degree to which grammar schools and even comprehensives imitate public school mores. The aristocratic ideal yields, in practice, to a simple defence of privileged roads to the top against the floodtide of meritocracy. Yet on the theoretical plane, a concern for cultural excellence, and resistance to the encroachments of vocational education and its ideologues, which form much of the philosophical substratum of the conservative tradition, need to be integrated, in a new form, into any socialist educational programme.

The Rationalizers of the System

The second, and currently most influential, school of educational thought is a product of the expansion of education over the last 90 years. It could be said to express the aspirations of the fast-growing new middle-classes, above all the technicians and white-collar workers, who chafe at the closed, aristocratic hierarchies of British society, but whose horizon is one of an open merit-determined escalator—who in Britain, without a mass socialist party, have never been offered the possibility of a classless society. This outlook is represented at one end of an ideological spectrum by the official reports—Newsom, Robbins—and by Vaizey(11); at the other by Floud and Halsey.(12) It is, above all, concerned with the organizational modalities of the school system. It denounces its inadequacies and inflexibility, the 'wastage' of its selection system and its excessive restriction of channels for mobility, its denial of equality of opportunity. Clearly the attack mounted by the most radical thinkers of this school on the inherent deficiencies of the present system, and their consequent powerful support for the reorganization of secondary education along comprehensive lines, does contribute greatly to the unlocking of the present situation, and has a significant overlap with socialist demands as such. But this approach does not intrinsically transcend the limits of a modernizing, propulsive neo-capitalism. It offers no serious challenge to the present content and values of British education. When Halsey, for example, does try to come to grips with the content of education, in his essay *British universities and intellectual life*(13), his radicalism collapses ignominiously before the most vulgar myths of ruling class ideology: 'Educationally they (Oxford and Cambridge) have stood for a broad humanism against a narrow professionalism, for 'education' as opposed to 'training' ' and again: 'The success of Britain as an imperial power in the 19th century and especially the quiet and incorruptible efficiency of its high ranking civil servants and colonial administrators commanded universal *(sic)* esteem and was at the same time a powerful validation of its educational institutions and the high values placed within them on classical studies and the liberal arts.'

Comprehensive education, if it remains streamed, is only a rationalized form of the present tripartite system.(14) But once it is realized that the same arguments which have been marshalled against the tripartite system on the grounds of built-in class bias and the self-fulfilling character of 'intelligence tests' apply equally well to streaming, then the whole concept of education comes into question, since unstreamed classes involve profound changes in teaching methods,(15) changes in teachers' training, and above all changes in curriculum.

At the same time, those thinkers who have been most concerned with the rationalization of the educational system have also been the strongest advocates of educational expansion. A socialist programme here coincides with the objectives of the modernizers; but it must give expansion a different meaning. For a socialist education should be designed to meet and develop human needs, and, as Raymond Williams says, to 'keep the learning process going, for as long as possible, in every life.'(16) Expansion divorced from such an aim can only too easily consist simply in a more highly developed system of vocational training, which relieves industry of a still greater part of the costs of training its new recruits, transferring this charge to the community.

Romantic Education

The third tradition springs from Rousseau, Pestalozzi, Froebel, and Montessori, and from Freudian psychology. Romantic, reacting against orthodox curricula and methods, showing great concern for the *individual's* self-realization, enriched in this century by the advances of modern child psychology with its emphasis on play and free expression, it could be said to represent the liberal wing of the bourgeoisie—its conscience. Whereas the readers of the *New Scientist* and of *New Society* might be expected to be overwhelmingly among the 'rationalizers', the readers of the *New Statesman* would probably be divided between rationalizers and romantics.(17) In Britain this tradition has produced no major educational thinker, but it gave rise at the beginning of the 20th century to a number of 'progressive' private schools such as Bedales, Summerhill, and Dartington. It has had its most important influence since the Second World War in the area of primary education, and in the 'failure' streams of secondary moderns and comprehensives. In so far as it has been responsible for the introduction of new teaching methods and for some kind of assimilation of modern child-psychology *anywhere,* it is of obvious human significance. It has also expressed an admirable resistance on the part of teachers to the 'rat-race' character of existing education and an affirmation of humane values against the inhuman priorities imposed by the economy. However, throughout its long history this tradition has failed to transcend its oppositional, escapist character,(18) and has failed to do more than salvage a minority from being broken by the system. It has been burdened by its acceptance of romantic conceptions of the individual personality which have reinforced rather than challenged the prevalent British orthodoxy stemming from Locke,(19) which sees each child as possessing *given* faculties which must be brought out by education. Above all, it has grasped only one aspect of the educational process—the provision of an environment in which children can grow as freely and creatively as possible. But it has conceived of this environment as an island within the englobing system, renouncing implicitly any aspiration to fight or even comprehend the system itself. Its curricular innovations have been limited to an adulteration of the old syllabus, with the introduction of some manual skills and a higher proportion of creative work. David Holbrook, who is representative of a vulgarized but typical and influential version of this school of thought, has encapsulated its inadequacy in the inimitable dictum: 'We need to restore to secondary education the poetic function—that poetic function which is the basis of all human activity.'(20) That the 'poetic function' is the basis of all human activity is clearly nonsense. What is true is that there is a real risk of its being made the opium of the lower stream children. It comes as no surprise to find the educational establishment unanimous in its praise for Holbrook and his brave work, as the Victorian bourgeoisie was for the work of the Salvation Army. The ever-present danger for this whole school of thought is that it can so easily be absorbed and used as a palliative where the system breaks down, thus becoming complicit with the very education it purports to challenge. However, it has given birth to most of the really original reflection on teaching methods. Its stress on play, on group learning, on flexible class-room organization, and its rejection of the traditional teacher-pupil relationship, are permanent contributions. Above all, it alone among the major traditions of educational thinking in Britain has accepted Freud. The great achievement of Freud and his successors in exploring the formation of the individual personality in childhood represents a fundamental acquisition, which must be pivotal to any contemporary socialist discussion. One of the most crippling failures of the socialist intellectual tradition in this century has been its failure to integrate either the romantic and anarchist 'moment'—except perhaps in the early years of the Russian revolution, or the Freudian oeuvre—except in the work of individual thinkers such as Sartre and Marcuse.(21)

The Democratic Tradition

The last major tradition is that of those thinkers who, in Raymond Williams' words 'made a generous response to the growth of democracy'—the tradition of Mill, Carlyle, Ruskin and Arnold in the last century, and of Williams himself in the 20th century. It provides the philosophical expression of the pressure towards universal education, as it now provides the overt ideology of the campaign for comprehensive education. But although the supporters of comprehensive education explicitly situate themselves in this tradition, there is often something rhetorical about their use of democratic arguments.. The logic of Vaizey's arguments in favour of educational expansion as a good capital investment reinforces the vocational conception of education, which is precisely the opposite of a democratic conception.(2 2) Similarly, Floud and Halsey argue against selective education on the grounds that it is not 'fair', thereby implying an acceptance of vocational purpose as the main purpose of the schools. In both cases, the 'democratic' formulations appear subordinate to, and in fact implicitly contradicted by, the principal argument in terms of life-chances.

Thus much of the educational thinking that purports to be within this tradition, in fact, tends in precisely the opposite direction. However, a democratic conception of public education holds out in the primary school syllabus, despite the prevalence of streaming and the downward pressure—ideological as well as practical—of selective secondary education.(2 3) It is also the rationale of adult education. Its theoretical weakness is potentially compensated by the untapped reserves of response to it among teachers, among parents, and among children. It is the tradition which underpins the comprehensive school despite the ideologies of the present campaign. In recent years it has received one major reformulation in the work of Raymond Williams. Since this represents the most ambitious and radical attempt by a British socialist to challenge the existing system, and to present an alternative to its curriculum, it deserves the most careful attention.

Williams, after a historical account of the development of educational theory and reality in Britain, presents a draft curriculum—which he suggests as a minimum standard for every educationally normal child:

1 Extensive practice in the fundamental languages of English and mathematics.
2 General knowledge of ourselves and our environment, taught at the secondary stage not as separate academic disciplines but as general knowledge drawn from the disciplines which clarify at a higher stage, i.e. (i) biology, psychology; (ii) social history, law and political institutions, sociology, descriptive economics, geography including actual industry and trade; (iii) physics and chemistry.
3 History and criticism of literature, the visual arts, music, dramatic performance, landscape and architecture.
4 Extensive practice in democratic procedures, including meetings, negotiations, and the selection and conduct of leaders in democratic organizations. Extensive practice in the use of libraries, newspapers and magazines, radio and television programmes, and other sources of information, opinion and influence.
5 Introduction to at least one culture, including its language, history, geography, institutions and arts, to be given in part by visiting and exchange.

He proposes that this could form a common education to the age of 16, when compulsory school would cease. Further education would take place in a variety of institutions, in which vocational training and general education could take place side by side, and in which students would participate in organization and control.

Certain of the stresses of Williams' draft are clearly of the greatest importance (it is not the intention here to discuss details of the suggestions). The stress on an integral and rational curriculum is a genuine attack on instrumental or vocational education. Science would be taught as it should be and never has been in Britain as an essential element of contemporary man's view of himself and his world.(24) The whole of contemporary culture and all the arts would be part of the curriculum.(25) It must also be clear that this programme implies the liquidation of the private sector, the end of tripartism and of streaming, of sex segregation and differentiation. It would involve a massive expansion and retraining of the teaching staff, an extension of the school career, and a reorganization of the universities. In short, it is a deliberately maximalist programme, and a good one. The immense merit and importance of Williams' proposals are evident. They represent the *only* authentic socialist programme for our educational system in Britain today.

But at the same time, this programme suffers from a fundamental weakness. Williams presents his draft as a reform which could be accepted by an enlightened society. There is no discussion of who could impose it and who would oppose it, and no reference to the concrete politico-cultural structure of Britain or the existing social composition and outlook of the teachers. Williams' fundamental mode of presentation is the rational appeal to people of good will. 'We can see a certain way ahead . . . the only sensible answer . . . We shall have to think in terms of . . .' This 'we' is revealing, for it clearly does not in the context mean socialists: ('We still think of required levels of general culture, according to certain classes of work'). It is based on some unspecified consensus in an extra-historical sphere. 'In terms of such a definition (referring to his draft curriculum) we could revise our institutions.' With any other writer one would see this as a singular mystification. *Whose* institutions? *Who* could 'revise' them?

Williams' whole scheme in effect hangs in the air, suspended in a kind of atemporal void. There is a basic failure to ground the proposed programme in any actual historical situation. Above all he completely overlooks the fundamental fact that a reform of the educational system involves a reform of the educators as well, and that this is a *political* task, which immediately ricochets back to the question of transforming consciousness and ideology throughout society. As they stand, Williams' proposals remain purely 'institutional', exhibiting a detachment from actual political reality, which can lead him in another field to suggest that the socialist solution for the capitalist press should be to transfer the papers to the journalists who work for them.(26) The idea that *Daily Express*—or for that matter *Times*—journalists, if they controlled the paper democratically, would produce a 'democratic' newspaper ignores the obvious fact that social institutions of this kind—schools or press—produce the people to fit them.

The corruption of the *human material* in each sector cannot be put in parentheses in proposing their transformation. It must enter into the initial determination of what the programme should be.

The Revolutionary Alternative

In other words, a socialist programme cannot consist of a purely *conceptual* alternative. It implies precisely the fusion of theory and praxis, and a rejection of the idea that socialism can be brought about by the simple advocacy of ethically superior policies, without a revolutionary movement capable of contesting capitalist society as a whole and prefiguring a new cultural order. Such an alternative would represent a junction of programme and strategy, of theory of human beings and of political action. Of course, to speak of such an alternative in Britain today is 'unreal', but it is only by starting to think in these terms that established reality can be challenged.

A socialist theory of education would resume at a higher level the valid elements in all the theories discussed above, combating and integrating them at the same time. It would be distinguished from each in precise, inter-related ways:

1 As opposed to the conservative tradition, it would stress education as the development of *critical* reason (in Marcuse's sense of the word) in the child—a

questioning attitude towards all existing reality.

2 As opposed to the romantic school it would embody a full acceptance of the *social* character of humanity, rejecting for ever the notion of a pre-social dimension of human existence—the image of Emile.

3 As opposed to rationalizers it would insist on the *active* nature of the child's participation in the learning process, and contest the mechanist conception of education as the transmission of fixed skills.

4 As opposed to the democratic tradition, it would be *dialectical,* treating all human reality as radically historical, refusing to consider programmes outside of men to execute, emasculate or refuse them.

Such a theory would consider education as an integrated system, and aspire to refound it in its totality. It would view education as process of socialization, as process of acculturation, as vocational training, as creator of intellectuals and culture; it would analyse it historically and sociologically, as an element in a wider society and culture, and as a world in itself with its own rules and values.

Above all, it would fuse analysis of the total system with a strategy for transforming it—a socialist theory of education with a programme for educating socialists.

With this, we return to the point of departure of this discussion: the fact that education can only be understood as at the same time provision for human needs and an element of the power structure. As such, a theory of education is central to socialist theory, and has been considerably under-estimated by the marxist tradition. There exists in Britain today one body of work in the field of education which brings this home very forcibly; it is genuinely revolutionary and any educational theory must integrate its achievements. This is the work of Basil Bernstein.(27) Bernstein's work implies that class divisions are consolidated at a very much more intimate level than is usually imagined, and that the schools serve to sustain the class structure by an exclusion of the working-class child from the culture of his society in the most radical and dehumanizing way conceivable, by alienating him in his speech—his elementary mode of communication with other people.

Once the dialectical unity of the task of transforming institutions and the task of transforming people is fully accepted, it can be seen that a central problem is that of the transformation of the teaching body. For the teachers in Britain are overwhelmingly conservative, not merely politically but educationally too. To think in terms of a socialist alternative in education is purely illusory unless this alternative includes the liberation of the teachers. This transformation could only take place within the practice of a mass socialist movement—so that the problem of the teachers immediately repercusses back on the general problem of creating a hegemonic socialist party with beach-heads in the teaching profession. Such a practice could only be founded concretely on demands which arise from the teacher's situation. The two moments must be held together: separated, they turn into the familiar sectarianism on the one hand and corporatism on the other.(28) Socialist education means socialist teachers, and the practice of socialist teachers can only succeed if it integrates the political struggle and the professional demand. Conversely, the socialist movement can only succeed in transforming education if its practice integrates the teachers, creating and recreating them as socialists.

References

1   'The returns on education, both individually and socially, are at least as high as those in physical capital. More important the development of the physical equipment of society may largely be wasted unless there is the trained talent to work it.' Floud, Halsey and Anderson, *Education, Economy and Society*. p.38.

2   It is important to stress in this context that the teachers are

predominantly working-class in origin, yet seven out of ten of them vote Conservative. They thus represent one of the greatest single successes of the dominant class in subordinating the working-class to its values.

3   *The Long Revolution* pp. 125-55. Raymond Williams.

4   Religion is the *only* compulsory subject in the State school system.

5   An excellent study of a similar phenomenon in French universities was published in *Temps Modernes* May 1965, by Francois Josse.

6   Some Effects of Streaming and Sex Segregation (unpublished PhD thesis Nottingham), J.C. Daniels. See also *Women,* Civil liberties pamphlet. 1965.

7   Antonio Gramsci: 'The Formation of Intellectuals' in *The Modern Prince.*

8   It must be understood that in the following sections there is an assimilation of very different thinkers which is at times brutal, for the purposes of the analysis. For instance, when Leavis is included in the conservative tradition in the educational context, this classification does not affect his very radical contributions in other fields.

9   Burt's work is fundamental to the ideology of 'intelligence'. The best demolitions of his views are those of Vernon in 'Bearings of recent advances in psychology on educational problems'; and of Daniels, op.cit.

10 *Education in an Industrial Society* pp. 118-19. *Education and Values* p.151.

11 *The Control of Education, The Economics of Education; Education for Tomorrow.*

12 Representative articles in Halsey, Floud and Anderson. See also Jean Floud, 'The Teacher in an Affluent Society', and 'Sociology and Education', Sociological Review Monograph No.4. It is worth noting that although Vaizey is apparently to the right of Halsey and Floud, in some ways he is more radical in his rejection of the *values* of British education, particularly with regard to public schools and sexual segregation.

13 Halsey, Floud & Anderson op.cit. pp. 502-12.

14 See D.N. Holly's study in *British Journal of Sociology,* June 1965.

15 Forum: Unstreamed Schools. Pamphlet 1964.

16 *The Long Revolution* p.147.

17 See Perry Anderson, 'Problems of Socialist Strategy', p. 270 in *Towards Socialism,* for a discussion of the readership of these journals.

18 It is significant that this tradition has frequently been allied in Britain with forms of pacifism and anarchism which precisely validate and generalize this unwillingness to confront the system.

19 *Some Thoughts Concerning Human Education.*

20 *New Left Review.* No. 11.

21 An extreme symptom of this failure was the acceptance by much of the left of the crass philistinism and conservatism of Makarenko—the Russian equivalent of Baden-Powell. He advocated the deliberate repression of affection: 'In some families it is a constant kissing and cuddling, constant endearments and expressions of affection, so constant, in fact, that one begins to doubt whether there is genuine love or merely an habitual game behind these outward manifestations. In other families you will find a chill sort of tone, as if all its members live separate lives. The boy comes in, addresses his father and mother rather coldly, then goes about his business as if there were no love between them. And only on rare pleasant occasions will you catch beneath these outwardly restrained relations a fleeting glance of affection that goes as quickly as it comes. This is a real son, who loves his father and mother.' He was brutally authoritarian: 'You cannot ban love, but neither can you permit people falling in love and marrying at 18.' He was a die-hard segregationist: 'I would get the girls together and read them a lecture on how girls should behave. And then I'd get the boys together. These I did not so much teach as I simply demanded of them responsibility for their actions and behaviour.' And he explicitly recommended the use by parents of what contemporary psychology calls the double-bind: 'In such a case you should never say: 'Never do that, it's bad',' but better put it this way: 'I know you wouldn't do that, you're not that kind'.' Finally, he was a firm believer in mystification: 'Premature discussion of sex with children must be avoided on further grounds: the child will come to look upon sex in a coarsely realistic manner . . .' See *Makarenko: His Life and Work.* And *Selected Pedagogical Works,* by Makarenko.

22 See *New Left Review* Vol. 32, 1967, for Gramsci's discussion of this point.

23 Streaming: *An Educational System in Miniature,* Brian Jackson.

24 *The Long Revolution* p.142-44.

25 It is interesting to compare the convergence in the USA of the romantic and public education traditions in the work of

Dewey, which had an immense influence over the whole educational system. Dewey took from Herbart precisely the idea of an *integrated* curriculum in which the subjects are conceived of explicitly as parts of a whole, each illuminating and relating to the others. This conception, either as such or in its subsequent developments such as in the notion of 'core curricula', was widely adopted in American schools. Yet at bottom Dewey's ideas were deeply conservative, and underlie the whole subsequent preoccupation of educational sociologists and philosophers in the USA with socialization, internalization of norms and values, etc.

26 *Communications.* Penguin Special. 1963.
27 'Some Sociological Determinants of Perception', *British Journal of Sociology* IX (1958). 'Language and Social Class,' *BJS.* XI (1960). 'Social Class and Linguistic Development,' in Halsey, Floud & Anderson op.cit. 'Linguistic Codes, Hesitation Phenomena and Intelligence,' and 'Social Class, Linguistic Codes and Grammatical Elements,' in *Language and Speech* No. 5, 1962. 'Family Pole Systems, Socialization and Communication', paper given at the Conference on Cross-cultural Research into Childhood and Adolescence, University of Chicago 1964. 'A Socio-Linguistic Approach to Social Learning,' in Penguin *Survey of the Social Sciences* 1965.
28 A particularly important contribution on this question is that of Marc Kravetz: 'Naissance d'un Syndicalisme Etudiant', *Temps Modernes,* February 1964. 'De l'Algérie à la Réforme Fouchet: Critique du Syndicalisme Etudiant', *Temps Modernes* April and May 1965. Kravetz discusses the theoretical problems raised by the experience of an attempt to transform the UNEF (French students union) from a state of acute but essentially moralistic political opposition to the Algerian war into a revolutionary organization, by classical trade union means—the posing of concrete demands based on the students' work and life situation—and at the same time by an attempt to integrate it into a wider political practice.

Part Two

Class and Culture

Introduction

'There are times when you have to choose between being human and having good taste.'   *Bertolt Brecht*

What are middle class teachers doing teaching working class children? This is the dilemma facing many teachers. The answer could be made to fit into any of Hoare's four ideological categories, or any combination of the four, and still remain unsatisfactory. The fifth—his 'revolutionary alternative'—presents problems too; not the least of which is its almost complete absence from educational discussion and practice.

The theoretical background to such a discussion lies in the concept of culture and its relationship to class society.

Engels, in the extract which follows, shows that the cultural products of bourgeois society do not only serve the bourgeoisie—especially when they can be approached by working class people through their own independent institutions, for example working men's clubs putting on productions of Shakespeare.(1) The move towards compulsory state education can be seen as a way of counteracting and suppressing those working class 'schools and reading-rooms' which Engels refers to.

Independent working class education became a reality again in this country at the beginning of the century with the founding of the Central Labour College, in opposition to the so-called working class institution of Ruskin College.

But what about the concept of working class culture or art? After the Russian Revolution, an organisation called 'The Prolet-Cult' was set up. In 1921 it had 300,000 members and its aim was to introduce organisation—i.e. consciousness and plan—into the fashioning of proletarian culture, the elements of which are arising spontaneously wherever ideas and feelings are developing on the basis of collective labour. The Prolet-Cult arranges its programmes of activity in such a way that the proletariat can equip itself with new knowledge, express its emotions through new art, and transform its social relations in a real proletarian spirit—i.e. in the spirit of collective collaboration in labour.

Valerian Poliansky, the Chairman of the All-Russian Council of Proletarian Culture, continues: 'The proletariat must create its own class culture, which, in the future, when Communist society has been built up and classes have disappeared, will become the culture of humanity at large.'(2)

This is the issue Trotsky takes up in his speech on 'Class and Art': Can you talk about proletarian culture in the same way as you talk about bourgeois culture?

Another major issue Trotsky raises is the relationship between political orientation and artistic quality. When he says, 'One cannot approach art as one can politics', he raises the vexed question of political commitment in art. This was the debate that took place in the 'twenties between Lukacs on the one hand and Brecht and Benjamin on the other. Lukacs thought political commitment to the working class struggle could be developed through the traditional realism of the nineteenth century (e.g. the novel); whereas Brecht and Benjamin were looking for new techniques and forms of expression (e.g. films, newspapers, epic theatre) and new modes of production.(4)

There are many other writers too who discuss this tension between aesthetics and politics.   (See note 5 for further readings)

References

1 John Taylor, 'From Self-Help to Glamour: the Working Man's Club, 1860-1972,' *History Workshop*, Ruskin College, Oxford.

2 *The Plebs* Vol XIII No. 1 January 1921.

3 Leon Trotsky, *On Literature and Art*, Pathfinder Press 1970.

4 Georg Lukacs, *Writer and Critic*, Merlin 1970.
Bertolt Brecht, *The Messingkauf Dialogues*, Methuen 1965.
Walter Benjamin, *Illuminations*, Cape 1970.

5 **Suggested Readings**
Christopher Caudwell, *Beauty: A Study in Bourgeois Aesthetics*, in 'Further Studies in a Dying Culture', Monthly Review Press 1971.
Jean-Paul Sartre, *What is Literature?* Methuen 1949.
Herbert Marcuse, 'Art and Revolution', in *Counter-Revolution and Revolt*, Allen Lane 1972.
Shulamith Firestone, 'Sex Dialectics of Cultural History', in *The Dialectic of Sex*, Cape 1971.
Sheila Rowbotham, 'Through the Looking-Glass', in *Woman's Consciousness, Man's World*, Penguin 1973.
Louis Kampf & Paul Lauter, *The Politics of Literature*, Vintage Books 1973.
Perry Anderson, 'Components of the National Culture', in ed.
A Cockburn & R Blackburn, *Student Power*, Penguin 1969.
Arnold Kettle, 'The Progressive Tradition in Bourgeois Culture', in ed.
L Baxandall, *Radical Perspectives in the Arts*, Penguin 1972.
John Berger, *Ways of Seeing*, Penguin 1971.
Michael Rosen, 'Doing Eng. Lit.', in ed.
T Pateman, *Counter Course*, Penguin 1972.
Trevor Pateman, 'Impossible Discourse', in *Language, Truth and Politics*, Stroud and Pateman, 1975.
Paul O'Flinn, *Them and Us in Literature*, Pluto Press 1975.

Extract from The Condition of the Working Class in England
Friedrich Engels, 1845

These different sections of working-men, often united, often separated, Trades Unionists, Chartists, and Socialists, have founded on their own hook numbers of schools and reading-rooms for the advancement of education. Every Socialist, and almost every Chartist institution, has such a place, and so too have many trades. Here the children receive a purely proletarian education, free from all the influences of the bourgeoisie; and, in the reading-rooms, proletarian journals and books alone, or almost alone, are to be found. These arrangements are very dangerous for the bourgeoisie, which has succeeded in withdrawing several such institutes, 'Mechanics' Institutes', from proletarian influences, and making them organs for the dissemination of the sciences useful to the bourgeoisie. Here the natural sciences are now taught, which may draw the working-men away from the opposition to the bourgeoisie, and perhaps place in their hands the means of making inventions which bring in money for the bourgeoisie; while for the working-man the acquaintance with the natural sciences is utterly useless *now* when it too often happens that he never gets the slightest glimpse of Nature in his large town with his long working-hours. Here Political Economy is preached, whose idol is free competition, and whose sum and substance for the working-man is this, that he cannot do anything more rational than resign himself to starvation. Here all education is tame, flabby, subservient to the ruling politics and religion, so that for the working-man it is merely a constant sermon upon quiet obedience, passivity, and resignation to his fate.

The mass of working-men naturally have nothing to do with these institutes, and betake themselves to the proletarian reading-rooms and to the discussion of matters which directly concern their own interests, whereupon the self-sufficient bourgeoisie says its *Dixi et Salvavi*,(1) and turns with contempt from a class which 'prefers the angry ranting of ill-meaning demagogues to the advantages of solid education'. That, however, the working-men appreciate solid education when they can get it unmixed with the interested cant of the bourgeoisie, the frequent lectures upon scientific, aesthetic, and economic subjects prove which are delivered especially in the Socialist institutes, and very well attended. I have often heard working-men, whose fustian jackets scarcely held together, speak upon geological, astronomical, and other subjects, with more knowledge than most 'cultivated' bourgeois in Germany possess. And in how great a measure the English proletariat has succeeded in attaining independent education is shown especially by the fact that the epoch-making products of modern philosophical, political, and poetical literature are read by working-men almost exclusively. The bourgeois, enslaved by social conditions and the prejudices involved in them, trembles, blesses, and crosses himself before everything which really paves the way for progress; the proletarian has open eyes for it, and studies it with pleasure and success. In this respect the Socialists, especially, have done wonders for the education of the proletariat. They have translated the French materialists, Helvétius, Holbach, Diderot, etc., and disseminated them, with the best English works, in cheap editions, Strauss' 'Life of Jesus' and Proudhon's 'Property' also circulate among the working-men only. Shelley, the genius, the prophet, Shelley, and Byron, with his glowing sensuality and his bitter satire upon our existing society, find most of their readers in the proletariat; the bourgeoisie owns only castrated editions, family editions, cut down in accordance with the hypocritical morality of today. The two great practical philosophers of latest date, Bentham and Godwin, are, especially the latter, almost exclusively the property of the proletariat; for though Bentham has a school within the Radical bourgeoisie, it is only the proletariat and the Socialists who have succeeded in developing his teachings a step forward. The proletariat has formed upon this basis a literature, which consists chiefly of journals and pamphlets, and is far in advance of the whole bourgeois literature in intrinsic worth.

Reference

1 *Dixi et salvavi animam meam:* I have spoken and saved my soul.

A Worker Questions History
Bertolt Brecht

Who built Thebes, with its seven gates?
In books we find the names of Kings.
Did the kings drag along the lumps of rock?
And Babylon, many times destroyed —
Who rebuilt it so many times?
Where did the builders of glittering Lima live?
On the evening, when the Chinese Wall was finished,
Where did the masons go?
Great Rome is full of triumphal arches —
Who erected them?
Who did the Caesars conquer?
Did the inhabitants of famed Byzantium
All live in palaces? Even in legendary Atlantis,
When the sea swallowed it up, the drowning
Howled in the night for their slaves.

Young Alexander conquered India.
On his own?
Caesar beat the Gauls
Didn't he at least have a cook with him?
Philip of Spain wept when his fleet
Was destroyed. Did no one else weep?
Frederick the Second won the Seven Years War.
Who else won it?

Every page a victory.
Who cooked the victory feast?
Every ten years a great man.
Who paid the cost?

So many statements,
So many questions.

Class and Art*
Leon Trotsky

If I say that the importance of *The Divine Comedy* lies in the fact that it gives me an understanding of the state of mind of certain classes in a certain epoch, this means that I transform it into a mere historical document, for, as a work of art, *The Divine Comedy* must speak in some way to my feelings and moods. Dante's work may act on me in a depressing way, fostering pessimism and despondency in me, or, on the contrary, it may rouse, inspire, encourage me . . . This is the fundamental relationship between a reader and a work of art. Nobody, of course, forbids a reader to assume the role of a researcher and approach *The Divine Comedy* as merely a historical document. It is clear, though, that these two approaches are on two different levels, which, though connected, do not overlap.

How is it thinkable that there should be not a historical but a directly aesthetic relationship between us and a medieval Italian book? This is explained by the fact that in class society, in spite of all its changeability, there are certain common features. Works of art developed in a medieval Italian city can, we find, affect us too. What does this require? A small thing: it requires that these feelings and moods shall have received such broad, intense, powerful expression as to have raised them above the limitations of the life of those days. Dante was, of course, the product of a certain social milieu. But Dante was a genius. He raised the experience of his epoch to a tremendous artistic height. And if we, while today

* (This is an extract from a speech made at a discussion meeting called by the Press Department of the Central Committee of the Communist Party on May 9, 1924.)

approaching other works of medieval literature merely as objects of study, approach *The Divine Comedy* as a source of artistic perception, this happens not because Dante was a Florentine petty bourgeois of the thirteenth century but, to a considerable extent, in spite of that circumstance.

Let us take, for instance, such an elementary psychological feeling as fear of death. This feeling is characteristic not only of man but also of animals. In man it first found simple articulate expression, and later also artistic expression. In different ages, in different social milieus, this expression has changed, that is to say, men have feared death in different ways. And nevertheless what was said on this score not only by Shakespeare, Byron, Goethe, but also by the Psalmist, can move us. (Exclamation by Comrade Libedinsky.) Yes, yes, I came in at the very moment when you, Comrade Libedinsky, were explaining to Comrade Voronsky in the terms of elementary political instruction (you yourself put it like that) about the variation in feelings and states of mind in different classes. In that general form it is indisputable.

However, for all that, you won't deny that Shakespeare and Byron somehow speak to your soul and mind. (Libedinsky: 'They will soon stop speaking.') Whether it will be soon, I don't know, but undoubtedly a time will come when people will approach the works of Shakespeare and Byron in the same way as we approach most poets of the Middle Ages, that is, exclusively from the standpoint of scientific-historical analysis. Even sooner, however, will come the time when people will stop seeking in Marx's *Capital* for precepts for their practical activity, and *Capital* will have become merely a historical document, together with the programme of our party. But at present we do not yet intend to put Shakespeare, Byron, Pushkin in the archives, and we will continue to recommend them to the workers.

One cannot approach art as one can politics, not

because artistic creation is a religious rite or something mystical, as somebody here ironically said, but because it has its own laws of development, and above all because in artistic creation an enormous role is played by subconscious processes—slower, more idle and less subjected to management and guidance, just because they are subconscious. It has been said here that those writings of Pilnyak's which are closer to communism are feebler than those which are politically farther away from us. What is the explanation? Why, just this, that on the rationalistic plane Pilnyak is ahead of himself as an artist. To consciously swing himself round on his own axis even only a few degrees is a very difficult task for an artist, often connected with a profound, sometimes fatal crisis. And what we are considering is not an individual or group change in creative endeavour, but such a change on the class, social scale. This is a long and very complicated process.

When we speak of proletarian literature not in the sense of particular more or less successful verses or stories, but in the incomparably more weighty sense in which we speak of bourgeois literature, we have no right to forget for one moment the extraordinary cultural backwardness of the overwhelming majority of the proletariat. Art is created on the basis of a continual everyday, cultural, ideological interrelationship between a class and its artists. Between the aristocracy or the bourgeoisie and their artists there was no split in daily life. The artists lived, and still live, in a bourgeois milieu; breathing the air of bourgeois salons, they received and are receiving hypodermic inspirations from their class. This nourishes the subconscious processes of their creativity.

Does the proletariat of today offer such a cultural ideological milieu, in which the new artist may obtain, without leaving it in his day-to-day existence, all the inspiration he needs while at the same time mastering the procedures of his craft? No, the working masses are culturally extremely backward; the illiteracy or low level of literacy of the majority of the workers presents in itself a very great obstacle to this. And above all, the proletariat, insofar as it remains a proletariat, is compelled to expend its best forces in political struggle, in restoring the economy, and in meeting elementary cultural needs, fighting against illiteracy, lousiness, syphilis, etc. Of course, the political methods and revolutionary customs of the proletariat can also be called its culture; but this, in any case, is a sort of culture which is destined to die out as a new, real culture develops. And this new culture will be culture all the more to the extent that the proletariat has ceased to be a proletariat, that is, the more successfully and completely socialist society develops.

Literature Will Be Scrutinised
Bertolt Brecht

Those who wrote, sitting on gilded chairs,
Will be questioned about those who
Wove their coats.
Not for their lofty thoughts
Will their books be scrutinised, but
Some casual statement which discloses
Aspects of the weavers' lives
Will be read with interest, revealing traces
Of our famous ancestors.

Whole fields of literature
Written in choice phrases
Will be scrutinised for signs
That then too there were rebels in the midst of
    oppression.
Fervent appeals to supernatural beings
Will prove that mortals sat in judgement over mortals.
Exquisite harmony of words will only show
That for many then there was nothing to eat.

In this new age they will be acclaimed
Those who wrote, sitting on the bare ground,
Those who sat amongst the poor
Those who sat with people who struggled
Those who told of the sufferings of the poor
Those who told of the deeds of people who struggled,
Told artistically in the noble language
Formerly reserved
For glorifying Kings.

Their accounts of abuses and their appeals
Will still bear the imprint
Of the poor. For to them

Were they delivered, they
Carried them on under their sweat-soaked shirts
Through police cordons
To their own people.

Yes, there will come a time when
These clever, friendly,
Angry, hopeful people
Who wrote, sitting on the bare ground,
Surrounded by the poor and struggling
Will be publicly acclaimed.

Part Three

The Meaning of Literacy

Introduction

I lived in Stratford in a flat in Jupp Road. One Christmas we were going to move round the corner down Lett Road. It was about six years ago and we lived in Lett Road for a year. It was like Noah's Ark. We had a debris over the back garden and a little kitchen. A carpet lay on the floor and when you opened the street door it would blow up in the air. We had rats which ran about the house. My bedroom was downstairs next door to the living room. Once my brother was in bed and he had ants all in his bed climbing all over his face. He did not know they were there. He went to get a drink of water and there was one on his mouth. When I was seven years old there was a church across the road. In there was like an adventure playground. There were two cars, one on top of the other. You could climb to the top of it and swing all the way down. One mate of my brother's got a moped and rode it about in there. But the best bit was when the church got burned down. It went like a bomb. One year there were fireworks. It was the fifth of November. A telegraph pole was put upright and all wood and paper, anything that would burn. It was good. Someone got burned. In the primary school I had the cane once a day. When I was eight I moved to Plaistow. I've been living there eight years this summer holidays.

This is the sum total of a fourteen year old boy's written work in English during a whole year in a Newham comprehensive school. (The spelling has been corrected and punctuation inserted.) He was considered illiterate.

Put it alongside these statistics reported in October 1975: 'In Newham there are 88,000 dwellings. One third are council owned; 20,060 dwellings have no bath or shower; 23,000 have no inside toilet; 14,000 have no proper hot water system. There are 400 empty council flats and houses, and 6,600 families on the waiting list.' ('Fight Back Against the Cuts')

Compare a similar piece by a thirteen year old boy from a Secondary Modern school. Again this was virtually all he wrote in a year.

One night Butch and I left my house at ten o'clock. I always go up to the lights (our meeting place). We always go past the park. We got to the main gates of the park when a copper stopped in a panda car. He called us over and got out of his car. He asked us to turn out our pockets. I asked him why. He said once again, 'Turn out your pockets,' (with a bit more tone this time). So I said, 'Oh, I'm bloody going.' He told me to come back. I walked back slowly. He told Butch to go on home, so he went. He turned to me again and asked for my address. He told me to get in the car and took me home. As soon as my dad saw the copper he said to me, 'Get inside. I'll see you later.' My dad stood at the door with the copper for about five minutes. I was scared. My dad came in and said to me, 'BLOODY COPPERS!'

What do we make of these pieces of writing? At the very least they point to the feeling of oppression that children can experience in family, school and society; and this feeling is surely connected with the meaning they attach to literacy. This is why Wayne O'Neil makes the case for not 'pushing reading into context-less space' and so destroying coherence.

The question then is—what in the school curriculum and method of teaching takes account of the experience expressed in this writing? For it contains the seeds of most subjects in the school curriculum and many more besides. To start with the students' own experience is the method Paulo Freire has used in teaching adult illiterates in Brazil and Chile.(1) There, however, many of the peasants have had no opportunity of going to school to learn to read and write. Here it is the school system which produces adult illiterates.

The following passage is by a thirteen year old girl from a comprehensive school.

My earliest memories were of being continuously threatened, being told so much what I couldn't do that I became very bored. I hated going anywhere with my mother because I was always in the way, so it seemed. You must admit it's not much fun being dragged along to the post office or a large department store which hasn't any toys to look at. I'll never forget being taken into a waiting room of some kind where everyone sat in silence staring at you. My mother said to me, 'Keep still or I'll smack you in front of all these people.' I remember hating her for it and though it may seem just a little thing it haunted me continuously. I never forgot how those dreadful people stared. When you are young you can't defend yourself. When you are five or six, people think you enjoy yourself. I didn't. I longed to grow up and get out of this cage. Maybe that explains why now if anybody accuses me of something, especially my mother, I always argue over it. Sometimes I think mothers enjoy telling off their children and smacking them in public. They don't realise they have feelings too. My next memories were of my early schooldays which I hated. I started school at four and remember being asked what eight and eight equals in front of the class. I just cried, as I did every day. All the teachers picked on me and my best friend too. When she left I was lost. Her mother used to take me to school. All the girls in my class were nice to me and I had lots of friends, but I still missed her.

She was a talented, literate girl who could easily have gone on to do 'A' level English; yet, in her third year at secondary school, she didn't turn up at school for more than a few months during the year.

What the passage reveals is that the 'authentic dialogue between teachers and learners', which Freire writes about, seems never to have taken place, and the over-riding impression is of the frustrating sense of powerlessness which she feels. Bertolt Brecht illustrates this in his poem, 'In Praise of Learning', where he encourages the mad, the imprisoned, the housebound women, the aged, to learn and take power. He should also have included thirteen year old girls!

References

1 Paulo Freire, *Pedagogy of the Oppressed*, Herder & Herder 1968.
Paulo Freire, *Education: The Practice of Freedom*, Writers and Readers Publishing Cooperative, 1976.

Properly Literate
Wayne O'Neil

Political observations

In Bolivia, we are told, the government's anti-American campaign fails because the population is largely illiterate. In Vietnam repeated bombing and destruction of villages, crops, and land laid waste by chemicals and fire, a sporadic Song My, all turn an illiterate people away from the central Saigon government and the Americans—if indeed it has ever been turned in that direction—towards the Provisional Revolutionary Government and the Viet Cong. Actions read louder than words—if you can't read. Hausas depend on physiognomy, names, and Ibo-accented Hausa and English to pick and choose their Ibo victims.

Being able to read is not a necessary part of being civilized or uncivilized, useful or useless. One can hate or kill with it or without it. In fact, a nation can kill better with it—no argument for phonics or look-say.

Case Studies

I have known but two illiterate adult Americans.

1 Potters

One was an ancient, a Mr. Cole, North Carolina potter of a line of North.Carolina-Staffordshire, English potters as far back as memory reaches. He runs a prospering pottery shop in Route 1 just outside Sanford, N.C. He finishes a firing every two weeks, everything gone long before the next firing is out of the kiln. People come in and order pots of all sizes and shapes and he has them write their orders in a fat, black book. Too bad. He can't read. They never get their pots. So they learn to buy what he has or to leave a picture behind and get them back before someone else buys it.

He does well.

2 *Soldiers*

The other one I wrote love letters for. He was a wiry, young private in the U.S. Army who had been in civilian life a successful, well-paid steamfitter in the New Orleans shipyards. He could get into places other people couldn't. He got into the army because they promised to teach him to read. They didn't. Then he re-enlisted because they promised they would really teach him to read. They really didn't. They sent him to Germany. Somehow, though, in the midst of all this illiteracy his congressman got word of the broken promises and I was detailed to type all the love letters to his wife and family that he cared to dictate. (Presumably they could read, or maybe there was a civilian similarly detailed in New Orleans). It was embarrassing for both of us. Originals had two carbons; one to the congressman, one for our files. I hope everyone was embarrassed. Meanwhile he was being tutored on comic books. Never had to pull guard duty: he could easily memorize the general orders, but he couldn't read the special orders relating to his particular post in case the enemy should come to Gonsenheim.

I suppose he now reads as well as fits steam, or not so well—just comic books.

General conclusion

In the tangled, demanding revolution that is America, if you're illiterate you have no control or at most you have only limited control. If you can only read and remain illiterate, you're worse off: you have no control.

Make a distinction: being able to read means that you can follow words across a page, getting generally what's superficially there. Being literate means you can bring your knowledge and your experience to bear on what passes before you. Let us call the latter proper literacy;

the former improper. You needn't be able to read to be properly literate. Only in America and such like.

1 Schools
Schools render their Ss able to read—some of them—and in process destroy their proper literacy. Before they go off to school children have engaged in five years of bringing coherent (unspoken) explanations to the world of experiences, linguistic, social, etc., that they face. They're doing pretty well at it, too. The school tries to tell them, and generally succeeds in telling them, that common sense explanations won't do ever. It's really much simpler, the school says, experience should be understood linearly not hierarchally; it's all there on the surface, not deeply and complexly organized. Knowledge is a shallow thing.

1a Reading
The breaking down of proper literacy begins paradoxically enough with the teaching of reading. Sound-letter relationships are held to be linear and simple or else so mysterious and non-factorable that whole words are the thing. Children might just as well be going to a Koran school, learning to read backwards the Koran in Arabic. Reading is taught as if it were another language, another world, not as if it were a highly abstract representation of the language that the child already has tacit knowledge of. Intuitive connections are erased. And so is knowledge.

1b The rest
So it goes.

Lightly armed with his new, counter-intuitive way of dealing with experience and reading superficially, the child is now forced into re-viewing what he already knows and learning anew the surfaces of knowledge. Geography is reduced to a catalogue of names and capitals and products, history to a linear succession of dates and events, literature to a chronologically ordered set of the best thoughts man has best uttered—nothing of the systems of beliefs that underlie his uttering or the child's comprehending, nothing of what passes or doesn't pass from mind to mind. Science is reduced to taxonomy. Properly literate children are reduced to uncomprehending adolescents, improper literates.

Impropriety extends out of school into the real world. Improper literates buy newspapers, war, racism, male chauvinism, economic imperialism, and Nixon-Mitchell & Co. Improper literates run citizen school committees to prevent, *inter* alia, an Ipswich (Mass.) English teacher from exploring movement-youth culture beginning with a serious *Atlantic* essay and its serious, disinterested, lengthy analysis of the word 'motherfucker'. The real obscenity of Vietnam is condoned and supported, not understood. Honest attempts to understand obscenity in context are dismissed along with their teachers.

2 Something else?

Sure. Schools can build on not destroy a child's native literacy, on his well-developed ability to construct coherence around experience, to deal in words and actions with his experience. Learning to read is no huge obstacle to leap. Schools simply guard the chambers of the elite, throw up the barricades. Latin teachers hold out fear-of-the-subjunctive. All teachers have their subjunctive. Reading's the first. And most invidious.

Let them learn to read. Don't teach them. Let it emerge as they go about talking and telling of the riches they already possess. Forget word frequency counts. Who could work up any interest in the hundred most frequent words in any language? Keep all the words and the world together and them involved in it.

> Such involvement leads to a much more complete, comprehensive and holistic view of the life and world they are entering, and will put them more at home in it and in control of it.(1)

Pushing reading into context-less space is the first phase in the destruction of coherence.

Proper literacy should extend a man's control over his life and environment and allow him to continue to deal rationally and in words with his life and decisions. Improperly it reduces and destroys his control. He is deluded by the veneer of control he has been granted, not minding that he has lost everything else.

We have too much improper literacy at the expense of properly literate folk.

So it goes.

Reference

1 John H. Knowles, *Health in Vietnam and Urban America*, Occasional paper No. 3 of the Educational Research Center (M.I.T., 1969), 2.

In Praise of Learning
Bertolt Brecht

Learn the simplest things.
For those whose moment has come
It is never too late.
Learn the ABC, it's not enough, but
Learn it. Don't let it get you down!
Get on with it! You must Know everything.
You must take over the leadership.

Learn, man in the mad house!
Learn, man in the prison!
Learn, woman in the kitchen!
Learn, sixty-year old!
You must take over the leadership.
Search out the school, you homeless.
Secure yourselves Knowledge, you who are frozen!
You who are starving, grab hold of the book: It's a
   weapon.
You must take over the leadership.

Don't be ashamed to ask, comrade!
Don't let anything dissuade you.
See for yourself!
What you don't Know yourself
You don't Know.
Check the bill
You've got to pay.
Put your finger on every item
Ask: how did that get there?
You must take over the leadership.

Experience of Literacy in Working Class Life*
Peggy Temple

I want to be a bit more particular now and talk about my
own experience of working class life in two different
contexts. The first one when I was a child in a Norfolk
village 40 years ago, and what literacy meant in our
surroundings. I would say that we were working class, but
perhaps we had a rather uneasy position in the village
between the tradespeople, the vicar and our headmaster
and the doctor and the farm labourers at the bottom of
the scale who were regarded then as the lowest of the low
—who went to the Co-op to do their shopping and you
would never have been seen dead in the Co-op! But I still
would say that we led a working class life in general. My
father was a railway porter at a village station and later
on, a clerk, and later still a stationmaster but not 'til after
I'd left home, and he left his village elementary school at
the age of 13; boys from the country schools were not
entered for the 11+ or expected to go any farther, they
were destined to be farm labourers or something similar,
and anything they did beyond that had to be self-
education. We lived in a small house in the village which
was originally intended for farm labourers with one
kitchen/living room with a black grate, a small front
room that was never used except at Christmas and
christenings and funerals and so on, the front door was
never opened, but we did have books in the house. We
even had a bookcase in the kitchen and the book that I
remember seeing there was 'The Life of Maxim Gorky' in

*(Transcript of a talk given to fellow education students at NELP,
1975)

a red cover with the Heineman windmill imprint on it. Whether my father had read it, I don't know. I never did, but that's one I remember, presumably because of the name—names of people fascinated me. I remember showing utter disbelief when my father told me there was a film star named Clark Gable; I couldn't believe it.

And there was a big box of books under the bed in the back bedroom, the forerunners of paperbacks and Penguins, the Everyman cheap edition novels, and a Marie Stopes which I discovered and read under the bedclothes with a torch (laughter). And in the front room we had a big bookcase that was remarkable because it had no screws in it, we just pulled the glass front out and slotted it back and that was full of my granny's books, in quotation marks, which she willed to me when she died; Arthur Mee's children's encyclopaedias, countries of the world, a set of Everyman encyclopaedias and a whole lot of religious books because she was a divinity student, all with leather gilt tooled bindings—none of which I ever opened, but which still sit in that bookcase in my mother's front room. And one enormous one—'The Life and Work of St. Paul', about that size, by Dean Farrar, and they are still there.

But of course, when my Granny read, she read thrillers and books on Spiritualism and so on, and she introduced me to those when I was about 10 and it got to the point where I was too frightened to go to bed. But what undermines our status rather as a working class family was the fact that my granny was a teacher, but she came from Bethnal Green and she began her teaching life as a pupil/teacher at the age of 14 with 60 children in a class, but she did do what many of them in those days didn't, she went to college, St. Catherine's, Tottenham, and got her teacher's diploma in 1892. She went to Norfolk and became headmistress in various village schools, so I was familiar with school and books and things like that from an early age. When I stayed with granny the schoolhouse adjoined the school and I used to knock on the door and go into the classroom with the children as a baby.

Coming back to my own parents, my father was a great reader of magazines and newspapers; in those days Titbits and Answers with green and pink covers, The Daily Mail, The Passing Show, which gave coupons and you could get a set of Dickens from those. Our set of Dickens is in the bookcase in the front room. Some of them I read, but he read them all and he was reading Bleak House for the umpteenth time when he died. Now he liked non-fiction which I think would be true of many people of his age and generation in that situation. It was real to them, it described things that were actually in the world, experiences that they could have, and share, particularly he liked books about the war because he went to the first world war when he was 17, having added a year to his age, and while he was out in Mespot, as they called it then, he wrote a long diary of experiences. He wrote it in pencil and he rolled it up and we've never been able to decipher it to this day. Anyway, he wrote it. So I grew up with books (I must mention one or two others, I expect some of you remember Collie Knox, of the Daily Mail. That was another name that stuck in my mind and my mother used to make me cut out his column and I had to make them up into a scrapbook for her. And then there was Hannen Swaffer—I couldn't really believe that people had these names (laughter). We did Bullets in John Bull, the competition where you add the ends to phrases and if you're lucky you get a voucher to go in again next week— free. And then, when Picture Post came out, we had that from the first issue, and these things were talked about as well; I remember hearing people talking and discussing, oh, Amy Johnson, Jim Morrison and the Lindberg kidnapping, the Abdication and all those things). The first really political thing I remember is the Spanish Civil War and we had evacuees in our village and Franco was burnt on our November 5th bonfire on the village green.

That isn't really so long ago, but I haven't been able to find anybody else who knows anything about evacuees coming from that war to Britain, and I definitely remember that we had them; I even remember the name of one of the boys who came—he was a great footballer.

But anyway, from that childhood I became a reading addict, I read everything, from Biggles to books on Spiritualism. Jeffrey Farnol, Ethel M. Dell, Maria Correlli, and Limehouse Nights from the box under the bed. And I'm sure that the friends whose houses I went into had the same sort of reading habits, plenty of papers and magazines and comics always lying about and always a bookcase, however small, with some books in and other treasured possessions that may have been passed down.

Well, when I left and after two years at college, I went to teach in London, the war was still on and I was only 19, and it was a foreign country to me to start with, which I liked because I'd listened to my Gran's tales of Bethnal Green in the 1890's warning me against white slavery and things like that (laughter), and I'd always been determined to come. I began by lodging in Ilford in rather middle-class surroundings and here I would define middle-class as people who have dinner in the evening and not in the middle of the day (laughter), and having not much money—I think my first teacher's salary for part of the month of August was £13 out of which I had to pay back the college loan, so I used to go to bed early and read all the books in the public library. Again, I wasn't unhappy to do so, I enjoyed the reading. Then we were bombed out and I went to live with a girl from Old Canning Town, what you might call yer genuine working class, where bugs fell out of the roof at the old school in Bidder Street; I dare say she enlarged on some of the stories to horrify me and I was duly horrified but also fascinated. Our acquaintance developed from the book under her arm when she came to the school where I was teaching—it was Engels' 'Condition of the Working Class in 1844' and I scoffed at it. Then from that I was introduced to Jack London, another great author which the working class people have always enjoyed reading, and we joined a small political party and we sat about in basement kitchens in Hoxton, with slogans such as 'all men are liars' on the wall (laughter) and various bits of Marxist philosophy. We emptied the teapot out of the window, broke up a few more boxes for the fire and sat up all night, which is not to say that we all read these books, but there's a large number of the working class people who read them and read them well enough to discuss them. It was a university of a kind, no doubt biased, but an education in itself. On another occasion we sat in the back room in Upton Park, we were very cold, with a gas ring alight under the table to keep our legs warm, and amongst the things that we read and discussed —what was this—13,20,25 years ago?—Karl Popper, Schumpeter, Marx, Engels, Kant, Spinoza, Hegel, Sidney Hook, Wilhelm Reich, then later, there was deCastro's— 'The Geography of Hunger', Galbraith, Vance Packard, the more modern ones, and this is still going on in plenty of places amongst working class people, more and more I should say and more and more papers and magazines are being published by people themselves. Amongst the group that I knew there were many Jews and that ties in with another paper we had to read connected with literacy in the Jewish cultural tradition—and they certainly had a great respect for the written word and were great arguers, everything was a matter for contention and a good argument was worth sitting up three nights in a row for, and the many Jews in this group fitted in with a similar type of working class sub-culture of non-Jews, the gentiles, with no class, race, man, woman or bias of any kind that I was aware of at that time, and looking back I still don't think that I can see there was any bias then—we all met on equal terms; if you were ignorant, you were going to be instructed, and helped along. If you had anything to say, you said it. You went to the home of somebody who had a decent home, a fire to sit by, or you went to somebody's attic, it made no difference.

And now, just to touch on one more thing in the East End of London which a lot of people have already heard about—the enterprise which seems to be centred on a place called 'Centerprise' in Hackney, where I live, and Ken Worpole in particular, who was a teacher, but there's a whole group of people and it's going on in other places in the area as well as in Centerprise where local people are being encouraged to write their life stories, their poems, their novels, stories, schoolchildren as well as adults. In some cases they're taping it first and it's being knocked into shape or they're being helped with it by the people who work for Centerprise, but it's being published and it's being sold, people are buying it. It's not great literature—it's not meant to be, but it's enthralling and more and more people, having read other people's reminiscences are coming forward, the whole thing that Ken Worpole is doing is called 'The Peoples' Autobiography of Hackney'. He has also written books about the children's lives to be read in school; I found when I took 'The Hackney Half Term Holiday' to my classes, it wasn't local enough for them, that it would have had to have been a Newham half term holiday to really have appealed to them, because it was Hackney— another place, it might as well have been Timbuctoo or somewhere else—but the idea is good and there seems some purpose in all the covering of sheets with writing when it is to be published and read by other people, and not just handed round in school in duplicated form either. I feel that the working class culture is much more acceptable these days, but that even though it's tolerated in schools we're building on it rather than jumping on it, it's still much stronger in the oral traditions than in the written and the old wives' tales, the weather lore, the family saws, are still things which children are told. We sometimes regret they don't know nursery rhymes and so on, but I think it's surprising how many they do still remember in the face of so much that's poured out of television, radio and in comics which doesn't relate to this sort of undercurrent of culture.

And my conclusion is that the working class now, this vast generalisation covering the lot, compared with a hundred years ago, is literate, often highly literate and creatively so—most still choose only to use it for instrumental purposes, job, for information on their hobbies, to pull their motor cycles apart and so on and therefore they often prefer the typewriter and the telephone to the pen, but I still think there are far more children who take pleasure in writing than there were when I started to teach 32 years ago.

An Open Letter*

Dear Mr. Schmiederberg,

Is it true

that you have given up reading the newspaper during your lesson?

that your history teaching with Form 8A consists almost entirely of reading aloud from the text-book?

that you only stopped doing that when the headmaster was in the room?

that you have told parents of 8A that you make your lessons lively and interesting, even using films and discussions?

that these 'discussions' are rarely connected with the subject?

that you told 2 pupils as a punishment to do an account of the lesson and at the end of the lesson you took away their notes saying, 'There's going to be no writing in my lessons.'?

that you hardly do any written work?

that you sent a pupil in 10A out of the room when he wrote something on a sheet of paper?

that you did not let him take part in the lesson again when he was told to come back in by the headmaster?

that you try to discriminate against this pupil?

that now and again in this class you do not teach a history lesson but allow the pupils to do their homework?

that Form 10A is between 6 months and a year behind in history?

*From *The Megaphone*, a West German secondary school magazine produced by the pupils 1975.
After the publication of this letter, the headmaster tried to find out who had written it. When this failed he banned the magazine.

that when questioned you maintain that the class is keeping up with the syllabus?

Do not let these questions remain unanswered? We would be very grateful if you could convince us that you are after all a conscientious teacher.

The Editors

Part Four

Sexism

Introduction

Bourgeois society cannot see a woman as an independent person separate from her family unit and outside the isolated circle of domestic obligations and virtues.
Alexandra Kollontai, *Sexual Relations and the Class Struggle*, Falling Wall Press 1972.

I know the life of the worker, and not only from books. Our communist work among the women, our political work, embraces a great deal of educational work among men. We must root out the old 'master' idea to its last and smallest root, in the party and among the masses.
Clara Zetkin quoting Lenin, *Lenin on the Woman Question*, New York 1934.

We say that the emancipation of the workers must be brought about by the workers themselves, and similarly, the emancipation of women workers must be brought about by the women workers themselves.
Lenin, *Women and Society*, New York 1938.

Educational discrimination against women in the third world is clear from literacy statistics. In some African countries where 30-40% of the men have learnt to read, only 5% of the women have been given the same opportunity. Gunnar Myrdal's figures[1] for three Asian countries in 1961 were:

	Men	Women
Pakistan	29%	8%
India	41%	13%
Indonesia	57%	30%

In the west the discrimination is less a matter of access to education (except higher education) than of the form of education available. K.W. Berg illustrates this with reference to Scandinavian primary schools:

The traditional roles of the sexes are hammered into the minds of infant schoolchildren on virtually every page of every textbook they use, as has been pointed out by both Swedish, Norwegian and Finnish reviewers. The mothers work about the house, dressed in aprons, the girls too wear aprons, bake little cakes, put their dolls to bed, help their mothers and so on. Fathers—and sons—on the other hand are depicted in more variegated situations.

In addition to this, boys and girls are attributed different characteristics. Girls are invariably described as conscientious, dutiful, tidy and helpful, but at the same time passive and timorous. Boys are sometimes described aggressive towards each other, disdainful to girls, untidy and forgetful, but without any suggestion of reproach being made for these failings. Boyish pranks are acceptable, but one never comes across girls blithely contravening the rules laid down for them.(2)

This is the issue that Camilla Nightingale and Glenys Lobban take up in their articles on children's books in this country. Take a look at the Ladybird book, *Tootles the Taxi,* and see the boy on the tractor, the girl on the ground waving to him; the boy leading the girl into the caravan; the boy riding a bike while the girl stands on the pavement watching; the boy standing on the fence, the girl on the grass; the boy buying the icecreams.(3)

Or consider *The Vital Approach*, a book on English teaching by a Principal Lecturer in English at a Teachers' Training College. In a chapter on 'The Poetry Lesson', he says:

There is plenty of verse for junior school in which the child-experience is entered, but it is important to seek our similar explorations of the adolescent worlds—or of that part of the adult world which appeals to the adolescent. The little pleasures of home and its chores for future wives:

Coffee, be fragrant! Porridge in my plate,
Increase my vigour to fulfil my fate!

Monday was Washing Day,
Tuesday was Baking Day;
Wednesday h'Alfred 'as 'is dinner h'early. . .

Sure of a bed, and loth to leave
The ticking clock and shining delf.(4)

It is not surprising that 'Social Trends' 1974, the annual round-up of figures from the Central Statistical Office, concluded that education plays a significant part in keeping British women in a subordinate role.(5)

The argument in this section of the book is not that changing children's literature or altering the way women are referred to in our language will change our sexist society, but that sexist language and literature are examples of the way a sexist society operates, and that raising these issues and fighting on them are part of the struggle against such a society.

An integral part of this struggle is opposition to discrimination against gays. We have already seen how a gay teacher has been banned from employment with ILEA.(6) The results of a survey conducted by NOP for 'Gay News' show that, in reply to the statement, 'There are certain occupations that homosexuals should never be allowed to have like being teachers or doctors', 30% disagreed, 22% didn't know, and 48% agreed. One of those who agrees is the Chairman of the Croydon Education Committee who is reported as saying 'that if he were interviewing a man (no mention of gay women) for a teaching job who was known to be a homosexual, he would not appoint him'.(7) No wonder the NCCL report on gay teachers said that out of 48 education authorities, Croydon was the most bigoted. It seems likely that gay children have an even less positive self-image presented to them at school than do girls.(8)

A plan of action for feminist teachers is outlined by Glenys Lobban in her paper on 'Sexism in British Primary Schools'.(9) Her plan includes mutual support, self-criticism, achieving minimal competence in all the subject areas usually taught in the primary schools; raising the issue of sexism in class, staffrooms, union, rank and file meetings and parent teacher meetings; in-service education; and writing and publishing non-sexist texts.

The last point brings up the question of the availability of non-sexist materials for use in school. In America, a bibliography of recommended books about girls for young readers, called *Little Miss Muffet Fights Back*, has been produced by a group called Feminists on Children's Media.(10) In this country, the Children's Rights Workshop has brought out a list along similar lines, called *Children's Books,* which also includes principal references on sexism, racism and class bias in children's literature.(11) They have also recently published a collection of articles called *Sexism in Children's Books.*(12) CISSY (Campaign to Impede Sex-Stereotyping the Young) is another organisation active in this field.(13) They produced the children's books issue of 'Shrew', called *Goodbye Dolly,* and have been bringing pressure to bear on publishers.(14) The Leeds Women's Liberation group have been grading children's books on a five star system according to their freedom from sex-stereotyping.(15)

Another source of some children's books free from sexism is the Foreign Languages Press, Peking. *Little Pals* is a book for primary school children and shows a boy and girl both mending clothes, both cleaning their room, both shelling beans. *Little Sisters of the Grassland* is the story of two Mongolian girls, aged 11 and 9, who battle through a blizzard for a whole day and night to protect their flock of sheep. Similarly in *Secret Bulletin*, it is the girl who takes the initiative: she knows more about printing the bulletins than the boy; she thinks quickly to save him being caught, and she gets beaten in order to protect him.

Clearly this issue is only a small part of the whole area of sexual politics. A comprehensive stock catalogue on this subject is available from Compendium bookshop;(16) and a bibliography has been compiled by Sheila

Rowbotham,(1 7) which is also included in her book *Women, Resistance and Revolution.*

References

1   Gunnar Myrdal, *Asian Drama,* New York 1968.
2   K.W. Berg, 'Schoolbooks and Roles of the Sexes', *Hertha* No. 5, 1969, Fredrika Bremer Association, Stockholm.
3   Joyce Clegg, *Tootles the Taxi,* Ladybird, Wills and Hepworth.
4   Donald Mattam, *TheV ital Approach,* Pergamon Press 1963.
5   ed. Muriel Nissel, *Social Trends* No. 5, HMSO 1974.
6   *Gay Left* No. 1, Autumn 1975 — c/o 36a Craven Road, London W.2.
7   Gay News No. 83, November 1975.
8   Don Milligan, *The Politics of Homosexuality,* Pluto Press 1973
9   Glenys Lobban, *Sexism in British Primary Schools,* October 1974.
10 *Little Miss Muffet Fights Back,* Feminist Book Mart, 1974, available from Writers and Readers Publishing Cooperative.
11 *Children's Books,* Children's Rights Workshop, August 1974 73 Balfour St., London S.E.17.
12 Children's Rights Workshop, *Sexism in Children's Books,* Writers and Readers Publishing Cooperative, 1976.
13 *Shrew* Vol. 5, No. 4, October 1973.
14 Cissy Talks to Publishers, *Sexism in Children's Books,* 35a Eaton Rise, London W.2.
15 Newsletters Nos. 1-8 Children's Books — Women's Liberation Literature Collective, Leeds.
16 *Sexual Politics,* Stock Catalogue, June 1975, Compendium, 240 Camden High St., London N.W.1.
17 Sheila Rowbotham, *Women's Liberation and Revolution,* a bibliography, Falling Wall Press 1972.

Boys will be boys but what will girls be?
Camilla Nightingale

A critical look at children's books.

Ask any little girl what she wants to be when she grows up and she will say a nurse, not a doctor, a receptionist not a dentist, a secretary not an executive, an air hostess not a pilot (well why not a pilot?)

How many male secretaries are there? How many punch card boys? How many women occupy managerial positions? Why in these days of the pill and working wives are there still men's jobs and women's jobs, and why do the women's jobs offer so much less scope for advancement and fulfilment than the jobs for the boys? Why do girls set their sights so low?

Of course there are as many answers to this last question as there are typists in the Shell Centre. The short one: 'Girls are made that way', is too easy. A quick look at films, adverts, television and magazines, shows that many forces influence the way people think they should be. From the moment a baby is put in her first pink Babygro, she is being moulded into that creature of limited choices, a woman.

Some time after the pink Babygro, the little girl is presented with a book. From this and other picture books she learns a lot about the way little boys and girls are expected to behave.

She first learns about mother, the one person she will model herself on. Small girls are all the time shown in the house with mummy, helping her dust and sweep. Little boys help daddy with the things that he does, cleaning the car, mending the fence, painting the back door, making a bonfire.

Daddy never does mummy's work, like washing-up or making beds, and mummy never touches his car. Daddy is often seen reading a paper, watching television, going out or coming in. Mummy never reads, only watches television with a piece of sewing on her knee and never goes out by herself.

Print is powerful, and even children whose mothers are real ravers tend to believe in this passive pallid creature the books present. 'Why can't you be like a real mother,' they say as they play mothers and fathers according to the book.

The little girl also learns about play. When boys and girls play together in books (when the girls are not helping mummy) the boys can always run faster and climb trees better. Pictures never show a little girl ahead of a boy.

There is a picture in a *Ladybird* which is typical—of a boy at the top of a tree, and a little girl standing on the ground feebly putting one foot on the lowest branch. The caption reads something like 'We are climbing trees'.

At this age girls are often more physically advanced than boys, but already subtle pressures on them not to show it are building up in the books they read. Test this for yourself next time you are in Smiths or any bookseller. Go to the *Ladybird* stand and see if you can find any pictures where the boys are lagging along after the girls.

Naughtiness is important to all small children. A naughty child is asserting his individuality by rebelling against the rules. Boys have a monopoly on naughtiness. *Candy in the Tower* is ostensibly about Candy, but it is her friend Ginger who steals the scene by getting into scrapes. He gets his finger stuck in a suit of armour, and himself stuck in a cannon.

All Candy can do is try to persuade him to stay near the Beefeaters and be good. This is what she does, and it exhausts the poor kid so much that she falls asleep in the car on the way home. Ginger doesn't.

Remember *William* books? They were about a boy who was naughty, creatively naughty, all the time. All the girls I knew read them. Richmal Crompton knew this and tried to write about a female *willia*, and failed.

The different approach to boys and girls are shown in two books about the same subject. *Bedtime for Frances.* by Russell Hoban, and *Where the Wild Things are,* by Maurice Sendak, are both about children's night fears, Frances is afraid of a succession of things, she thinks her dressing gown is a giant and that nasty creatures will creep through a crack in the ceiling. Each time she is afraid she runs to tell her father, who patiently reassures her.

Max, on the other hand, flies off to the land of his monsters, fanged beasts who make terrible threats. He tames them single-handed and dances with them. There is a lovely picture of them all stomping and howling together before the monsters beg Max not to go away and leave them. Max confronts his fears and overcomes them triumphantly in true masculine tradition, while Frances has to be gently coaxed out of hers.

From their earliest picture books then, girls learn that they are expected to approach life in a different way from boys. In books, parents' roles are totally divided, in a way that exaggerates real life. I know lots of dads who wash up, put the kids to bed, and do the shopping, and I know lots of mums who read newspapers, go to the pictures, or even out to work. But you would think that this was a fact of life that had to be concealed from children. If a girl is tougher than a boy, she has learned by now to conceal it, at least some of the time, and she has also learned that naughtiness in boys is tolerated, even admired: 'Boys will be boys'.

By the time children are reading for themselves, these attitudes have hardened; 'Good gracious, it's those potty girls again', groaned the boy, 'Can't you leave me alone? You were talking a lot of rubbish yesterday and now you're talking it again'.

In any group, the leader is always a boy. Girls may be second in command but the crucial decisions are always made by the boy—'Julian's brow furrowed, and a thoughtful look came into his clear grey eyes . . .' The character who holds up the action by blubbing, or falling down a hole is equally certain to be a girl.

Adventure books written especially for boys have a far wider scope than those for girls. Boys' books are about subjects like trapping, sailing, smuggling, mining, the Wild West, cops and robbers. Scenes are set all over the world from Alaska to the South China Seas. The boy heroes need not only physical courage, they need to know what they are doing in great technical detail. Books like these are there to expand a boy's horizons.

Read a corresponding book for girls and you will conclude it is expressly designed to dampen down any spirit a girl may have left. They are set in ballet schools, and pony clubs, in the mild English countryside. The books are really about the social side of life, the only life girls are now supposed to be interested in.

Books are powerful. Everyone is taught to have some respect for print, and people believe what they see written down even when it does not agree with their experience. Children may not entirely believe that all adult women are the insipid mothers of their early books, or that girls are less capable than boys—after all they have only to look around them—but when the message is constantly repeated in all the books and magazines they read they cannot entirely discount it.

No books are written about women test pilots, deep sea divers or astronauts, and until this encouragement happens how can girls raise their thoughts higher than the typewriter.

Memoirs of a Suffragette
*June Kingston**

How I wish I could play a bigger part in getting the vote
for women. All I can do is join in with demonstrations. I
cannot say that I entirely agree with these demonstrations, and the attacks on other people and their property,
but unfortunately, there is no other way in which we can
achieve our aims. The Government will not listen to
reasoning, why should they bother if women want the
vote? they are all men. If we had a woman in the Government we could prove how capable we are of running the
country. We are as good as any man, and intelligent too.
Why should men get all the best jobs, and all the money.
I have to take part in demonstrations secretly for fear
that my husband will find out. He would surely beat me,
and probably throw me out of his house—His House! I
have just as much right to the house as he does. My
children are regarded as his children, my wages are said to
be his wages, as well as all my belongings, I have nothing.

My husband almost found me out recently. He said
that his friend had seen me breaking shop windows with a
toffee hammer in Regent Street. 'Of course,' he said,
'You would not join that group of faithless, cheap
women would you?' He said it in such a threatening way
that I was almost tempted to give up my fight for rights.
That was a good example of what we women have to
endure. I then received a lecture about how good he had
been to me, and how he had saved me from a boring,
poverty-stricken life and how he had given me a good
home to live in, and five beautiful children. That did it!
I was determined not to give up.

I joined in as many demonstrations as I could; I went

*secondary school student

to every meeting and each day I was more determined to see our aims through. Then something unfortunate happened. We were demonstrating outside the Houses of Parliament, and an M.P. called us 'Cackling hens, making a fuss over something that you will never achieve'. I found it hard to restrain myself, and I ran forward and hit him over the head with my bag. I was immediately grabbed by three policemen, and carried to their van in a very undignified manner. But I felt extremely satisfied, I was glad I had done it; until I was on the way to the police station, when I thought, God!, my husband will find out. I'm really done for now. I was tried, and, of course, found guilty and thrown into prison for three months. My husband disowned me, he was utterly ashamed of my behaviour and ungratefulness, he would never forgive me. I was past caring. I was not deterred.

I carried on with my demonstrations while I was in prison. I refused to eat any food. I was given a medical examination, very roughly, I might add, to see if I could survive without food, for some women are set free if they are weak, and liable to die if they do not eat. But I was declared healthy, and kept in prison. They did not do anything to make me eat my food. I suppose they thought that after a while I would give in, but I would not be beaten. But I grew paler each day, I felt weak, and I was sick frequently. They must have been concerned for me, because eventually I had to be force-fed. I was held down by two largely-built men. I was slapped round the face a few times because I tried to bite a large hairy arm, although I don't know whose it was. Then I saw the prison doctor slowly extending his arm towards my face. He was holding a long tube. I had heard of force-feeding before, how unpleasant it was, and every word was true. The tube was inserted up my nostrils, and a revolting liquid was poured down the tube. I choked and splattered, and the pain in the back of my nose got worse and worse, until I thought my head would burst.

Fortunately, I passed out, and saved myself from feeling any more pain. I was back in my cell when I woke up. The pain in my head was awful. I had to run to the basin to be sick three times during that morning. I slept for the rest of the day in fact, it was the best sleep I had had since I arrived. The bed was a wooden frame with a plank on top, and one blanket haphazardly sprawled across. I was glad it was summer, at least I did not have to encounter the cold nights of winter in a damp cell. There was one small wash-basin and a stool in the cell also, and a small window in one wall, so high up that even when I stood on the stool it was impossible to see out. The next day I awoke late. I even slept through the breakfast bell which was always rung at exactly 7.00am. The warden came into my cell with a small tray on which there was a mug and a small bowl. 'Here you are, come on get up, we've let you sleep long enough to-day, though why you deserve it I don't know. Come on, here's your breakfast.' Although I felt better than I had the day before, I was still longing for something to eat, besides if I carried on with my protest they would have to force-feed me again, and that I had to avoid at all costs. They let me walk round the prison yard for ten minutes the next morning, and I then faced another breakfast. I was very reluctant to eat it, but it was food, and I was still very hungry. Every day it was the same, a thin brown liquid, a broth it was called, with a few bits of meat floating around in it. Occasionally I was given tea or cocoa, without sugar, and it was so weak; but this became a luxury to me after a while. The first day I arrived my clothes were taken away, and I was given a thick ugly dress made from sacking, with my prison number badge pinned to the front. I was allowed to wash only in the morning, and bath once a week, in the same bath water that a few other girls bathed in. You were lucky if you were first!

Although I only stayed in prison for three months, it seemed like three years. The days and nights were long, and I was miserable and depressed. My only consolation was the thought that I was helping women by showing that I could stand up to the rough treatment as well as any man could.

When I was released, there had been no change in the situation. Government still would not agree to our wishes. But I joined in further meetings and demonstrations in order to help. I was even prepared to go back to prison! Fortunately, I did not have to, but many did, and some for longer periods than myself. But we believed it was for a good cause.

We are still without the vote, but I know we will get it one day, even if it is not in my life-time. Women, like myself and my colleagues, will not endure this treatment forever, there will always be women who admit that they are unfairly treated, and will do all they can to liberate themselves.

Sexist Bias in Reading Schemes*
Glenys Lobban

The subject of my talk tonight is Sexism in Reading
Schemes. Many of you will have seen Frances Rathbone's
article on this subject in the issue of *Shrew* devoted to
Children's Books. Possibly some of you will have seen my
own article on this subject in *Forum* (Spring 1974).
Hence I do not plan to spend too much time proving that
sexist bias does exist in readers. Instead, I shall
concentrate on two questions related to sexist bias. The
first concerns why it matters whether readers are sexist,
that is the way reading scheme content affects the
attitudes of children and especially girls. The second
question is what can be done to alleviate sexist bias in
reading schemes particularly.

Before I begin on the real meat of my talk, I will
summarize my own research findings. I coded the content
of six reading schemes (*Janet and John; Happy Venture;
Ladybird; Ready to Read; Nippers* and *Breakthrough to
Literacy*) and analysed 225 stories in all. I found that
there were far more male centered stories than female
centred stories. The activities of the two sexes were
rigidly differentiated in all the schemes. They all showed
a world where mum stayed home and did all the housework and all other domestic tasks, and where daughter
played with dolls and other expressive toys, helped mum,
and worried about her clothes and her appearance. The
male world was one where dad went out to work and did
handiwork at home, and where son played with
mechanical toys and was consistently more adventurous
and full of initiative than his sister. I concluded that the
schemes not only assumed female inferiority, and the

*Paper presented to the Children's Book Circle 18/3/74.

wife and mother role as the females' only 'proper' sphere of activity, they were about twenty years out of date. They showed a world more rigidly patriarchal than the one we have at present. Today many women do work outside the home and it is policy, in primary schools at least, for all children to do all activities from cooking to woodwork.

In my article I argued for a radical revision of reading scheme content so as to make it non-sexist and non-racist and to rectify its class bias. Two common arguments are often used to attempt to refute the call for a revision of the sex-role content of reading schemes. First it is argued that the schemes merely reflect the world as it is—the sexes are different and there you are. Second it is argued that the children do learn to read via the schemes and that is all that is important. Both these arguments are based on some fundamental misconceptions which need to be looked at carefully.

The first argument is that the schemes are not sexist at all but they simply mirror the real differences that exist between females and males. It is certainly true that our society produces females and males who are in general, very different from each other. Females tend to be less tough and aggressive than males, and their interests and dress are different from males. Females tend to see their prime function as being that of wife and mother. Males tend to be less capable of expressing emotion than females, and they see their adult role as that of bread-winner. Female and male children also differ from each other. By about age nine they have distinctly different interests and aspirations, *but* and this is the important fact, no researcher has yet produced evidence to show that any of these differences between the sexes (other than those of primary sex characteristics) are the results of biological sex differences. This means that the differences the sexes exhibit must be the result of their being differently socialized. Research shows that even tiny babies are treated differently according to their sex, girl babies are cooed at more often, nursed and cuddled more, and handled less roughly than boy babies. Thus by the time most children go to school they will have learned what sex they belong to and will show behaviour and interests that are sex appropriate. A child's experiences at school (as well as her/his learning via the media and peer groups) will probably serve to confirm her into being a 'proper' girl, or him into being a 'proper' boy. These later experiences might however question the role divisions the child has learned, and suggest that the child becomes a whole person who actualises her full potential rather than only half of it.

Reading schemes have an important role to play in this sex-role learning of young children. This role relates to the argument that all a reading scheme does is to teach reading. All the recent debate about race, class and, more recently still, sex bias in reading schemes has come about because it has been realised that readers teach more than reading. The content of a reading scheme and other books children read has a psychological effect, it influences the way children view themselves and the world. Reading schemes are thought to be particularly influential in this respect. They are often the child's first formal introduction to the written word, and they appear within the classroom and hence within the context of authority, and most children are compelled to read them. Researchers now argue that the schemes present a picture of the 'real' outside world for children and hence define acceptable and unacceptable patterns of behaviour and life styles. Children model their own behaviour and goals on that of the models like themselves who they read about in the schemes.

A reading scheme which shows rigidly different roles for the sexes (as all the schemes I looked at did) and which shows males as superior in everything except the ability to cook, dust, clean and smell flowers, has a profound influence on its reader. The implication readers will draw is that the sexes are, and should be, different. As children tend to copy behaviour of people like themselves and as what one's sex is is so often emphasized as important girls will tend to model themselves on the girls in the scheme and the boys on the boys, and hence each sex will tend to try out new behaviour that is 'correctly' sex-typed. The roles 'female' and 'male' are today becoming less rigid. Most women work outside the home, for example, and some men do stay home and take care of children. As I've said before, schools are supposed to encourage both sexes to do traditionally one-sex activities. None of these realities are reflected in most British reading schemes. Instead the weight of written authority presents decidedly the opposite picture. The schemes rigidly differentiate the sexes and show precious few role models for the girl who is tough and wants to climb mountains, or the boy who is gentle. Such reading schemes do not mirror real differences between the sexes, they are part of the process whereby artificial differences are maintained and perpetuated. Such schemes do not just teach children to read. They convey a subtle and pernicious message that females are inferior, and do untold psyche damage to the self evaluation of girls particularly.

You might refute my arguments by saying, but such sexist bias is a thing of the past and we all know about sexism today and new schemes will not show any such sexism. I wish this were the case. The most recent reading scheme to appear on the market is the MacMillan Language Project. I have nothing but admiration for the linguistic and artistic merits of this new scheme. The pilot pack which I inspected is glossy and interesting to children as well as educationally excellent and an interview with the editor in chief reported that the scheme purports to be unbiased. I made a brief content analysis of the pilot pack of the scheme and regret to report that there are more boy characters and more heroes than heroines and that many of the stories show stereotyped females and males. That this should still be the case in a scheme so linguistically excellent and one written so recently and with such care and self-consciousness is indeed depressing. It shows how deepseated are our sex-biases and how important it is that the demand for non-sexist content should be made loudly and publicly.

I hope my discussion up to now will have convinced you that it is imperative that something must be done to change and eradicate sexism in reading schemes (and other children's books). It is clear to me that books where the content denigrates females perpetuates a situation of inequality between the sexes. Such a situation means that neither sex is free to actualize their full potential. Content which contributes to such a situation is just not good enough. What then am I suggesting? I am calling for a revision of the content of existing reading schemes and I am calling on publishers to commission and publish non sexist books and schemes. Lest this clarion call sounds utopian I shall make certain specific suggestions concerning non-sexist content. A purely quantitative change would be for schemes to show equal numbers of female and male central and subsidiary characters. I would go much further than this quantitative change and call for qualitative changes in the treatment of child and adult roles in the schemes.

First let us think of children's roles. A reading scheme should show both sexes engaged in a variety of activities. They should show tough girls and tender boys (both of whom exist in proliferation) children of both sexes should be shown initiating all kinds of activities. It is important to note that none of these changes, though they might appear revolutionary if we measure the world by *Ladybird* standards, would diverge from actual children's experience in the class or with their peers. Hence such content could not be criticized on educational grounds as being unlike 'real life'. Also, children are dissatisfied with present unreal and rigid role divisions. For example, one of the girls in my class refused to read the Pirates scheme as 'there's no girls in them books Miss'. To illustrate my point I shall briefly compare two books I'd regard as sexist with two that are not sexist. The two sexist books I chose (from the infinity available) both come from the Nippers Scheme.

They are 'Lost in a Shop' (with a heroine) and 'John's First Fish' (with a hero). Comparing them is illuminating. Both books show the central character going off alone. The girl Jane, as the title foretells, gets lost in a shop by mistake. The boy, on the other hand, valiantly tries to save his young sister from drowning even though he can't swim. He and his sister then are sent to swimming lessons and he, surprise, surprise, turns out to be a champion swimmer. (It's his dad incidentally who teaches him to fish and his sister always just watches). The two non-sexist books I chose (out of the precious few available) were the *Nippers* story 'The Lost Money' and 'The Wendy House' from the *Breakthrough to Literacy* scheme. The boy in the first story posts his mum's money instead of her letter (a mistake anybody could make).

The important thing about this story is not this mistake, it is the fact that the boy is actually shown feeling worry and expressing his anxiety by crying. Many boy children do cry but this was the only story I found where the author was not so hidebound by the stiff upper lip ethic as to refuse to show boys capable of such behaviour and feelings. 'The Wendy House' has two main characters, a boy and a girl. They invite their friends (and their teacher) to tea in the Wendy House and both the text and the illustrations show both of them preparing and serving the tea. The story ends 'Now *we* have to clear up'. It is a pleasure to find books like these latter two, but unfortunately books which show both sexes as real people are rare in existing reading schemes, and such unstereotyped and realistic treatment of children's roles is what is needed.

The other area where qualitative change is needed is that of adult roles. Once again, equal numbers of female and male adults should be shown. Both females and males should be shown pursuing jobs outside the home, and the wide variety of jobs that are done by the sexes today should be shown. Why, for example, do schemes never show female doctors or male nurses? Any child unwise enough to base their assessment of the real world on the content of the six reading schemes that I analysed would conclude that all jobs other than those of housewife, relative, teacher and shop assistant were the sole prerogative of males. Thus once again the changes in content that I am suggesting are not unrealistic—such patterns exist in real life and it is the schemes which are unrealistic. Another important area where qualitative change is necessary is the tender issue of domestic relations. While it would be unrealistic for every story in a scheme to show both adults in a nuclear family doing equal amounts of household maintenance, many males do do housework and many females are competent handi-women, but stories seldom show such people. An excellent and amusing exception is the Language in Action story 'Thumbs Up'. The story begins stereo-typically with Grandad and grandson Tom in the shed doing woodwork while Gran knits inside. First Grandad and then Tom bang their thumbs and Gran bandages them in true feminine fashion. Page 13 rings the changes. We see Gran in the shed banging and humming while her menfolk sit inside holding up bandaged thumbs. Gran completes the go-cart and the final page shows her giving a thumbs up with a healthy thumb and a broad wink on her face. The story is simple and unmoralistic and true to real life. Stories which show the female doing all the housework and childcare might bring in the issue of the women feeling dissatisfied or disgruntled at this state of affairs which would again be supremely realistic. Another area of adult interaction that needs revision is that of marital bliss. Stories that raised such issues as parental fights, divorce, single parent families etc. were virtually nonexistent.

I hope that this talk has shown you that the present content of reading schemes denigrates girl children and causes damage to their self evaluation by accepting the society's designation of females as inferior. It also denies the full potential of all people for a variety of emotions and skills and presents a half world for each of the sexes. I am suggesting that it is absolutely imperative that we see a change in the sex-role content of reading schemes. I am not suggesting utopian books which present a view of the sexes as totally equal. The sexes are not totally equal as yet. Our society represses females and total equality will only come with radical social change. I am suggesting that reading scheme content does two things. The first is to reflect reality and show tough kids and working and nurturant adults of both sexes. The second thing I am suggesting is that reading schemes do not assume as they do presently, that present sex differences are inherent and fixed. The series should pose the question of sex-roles and sex differences and female equality. This could be done by, for example, showing girls fighting through to independence and Mums pissed off at the fact that they do all the housework and hold down another job. It is time that publishers and writers and readers realised the role present sexist reading schemes play in perpetuating sexual inequality and a radical revision of sexist bias occurred.

Does it really matter whether a man desires another man?*

'Does it really matter whether a man desires another man?' I asked. The party stared at me, amazed. Throwing them a sick smile to cover my question, I shut my mouth and remained silent for the rest of the discussion. What did it matter that a man loved another man or a woman another woman? Why should we be obliged to love the opposite sex? It was sick; I could have kicked myself for backing down. I wanted to ask the question again, but I felt outwardly ashamed, and inwardly insulted. Why couldn't I back my question up? All I did was to reflect their views.

'I suppose it's a weakness,' said Smith.

'They ought to be locked up,' said Jones.

The discussion ended, and I went home with my nagging question that needed an answer.

'Does it really matter whether a man desires another man?' I asked boldly of my mother.

'I don't know dear, I suppose so,' she said, drying the plates.

'You suppose that it does or doesn't,' I said, impatiently.

'What?'

'Do you think that it matters?'

'I'm sorry dear, what was it that you said?'

'Never mind,' I replied and went away in defeat, not daring to ask the question again.

'It seems obvious to me that there must be something wrong with them,' hollered Jones.

'Oh yes, I agree but. . .' said Smith, turning pink.

'But, but what? I can't see any buts about it,' shouted

* By a secondary school student

Jones.

'I don't think that it matters whether a man desires another man.' The whole assembly went quiet. I looked around, not believing that I had uttered the sentence. I remembered asking a similar question some years ago, and not receiving an answer. I felt panic stricken; they all just stared.

'You don't think that it matters!' I turned and experienced a thrill of excitement to see Jones, standing red in the face, glaring at me.

'You don't think it matters!' he screamed at the top of his voice, again.

I stood up firmly, trying to look as bold as he felt and looked.

'Why should it?' I asked calmly.

'My dear woman,' he said in a lowered tone, as he reseated himself. 'A man needs a woman to produce children.'

'Oh, I see,' I said, in an agreeable tone, 'that is the reason why another man cannot love a man and another woman a woman.' I smiled and waited for his reply.

'Yes my dear,' he said, gathering his papers together as if having settled the argument.

'Rubbish!' I shouted. 'Our sole purpose on this earth is not to produce children.'

Jones stood outraged. 'God put . . ' he started.

"God put,' he may have put you here but he didn't put me here to produce children,' I interrupted.

'Oh,' he said, more calmly, 'then what exactly did he put you here for?'

I stood blank, failing to see what he was getting at.

'To love another woman perhaps? Do you love another woman?' he asked, full of himself.

I stared momentarily in wonder, before adding, 'No sir, I do not.' Jones stood proud and looked around the assembly as if waiting for them to applaud.

'But equally,' I added, Jones turned and stared in

amazement, 'I do not love another man.' Jones gave an insulted gasp and seemed unable to speak.

'Good day,' I smiled and left the room.

Word Consciousness: Sexist Language and Attitudes
Kristine L. Falco

We often take our language for granted. Rarely do we reflect on the meaning of the words we speak. Rarely are we aware of the impact our words can have on other persons. This paper will explore some of the questions that come up when people become aware of their words, what they connote and how they affect others. First I will look at some ideas about how language might affect people's attitudes. Then I will explore how changing language might in turn change attitudes. The specific realm of language change studied here is the rampant sexism in our English language.

Does Language Affect Attitudes?

Linguistics have long debated this question. Many theories hold that attitudes create the language. Others maintain the opposite: that the language can shape attitudes. Benjamin Whorf believes that language habits '. . . are seen as determiners of social relations through their role in shaping the culture.'[1] B. Bernstein feels similarly:

> . . . a number of fashions of speaking . . . are possible in any given language and . . . these fashions of speaking, linguistic forms, or codes, are themselves a function of the form social relations take. According to this view, the form of the social relation or − more generally − the social structure, generates distinct linguistic forms or codes and *these codes essentially transmit the culture and so constrain behaviour.* (Emphasis his.)[2]

Bernstein believes that the language a child learns affects what she or he learns, how it is learned, and sets limits on what future learning is possible.

J. Faust feels that men have used language very effectively to oppress women: '. . . he knows the power of language. He knows that language can control not only behaviour, but thought itself.'(3)

Unfortunately, the above theories are just that: theories. To date, there is no conclusive evidence that language limits and colours learning. So, since I cannot claim that language creates sexist attitudes, I will explore the possibility that language solidifies and perpetuates those sexist attitudes in our culture.

Germaine Greer, referring to the pejoration of words over time and to the change-over of such words as 'witch' from its original bisexual meaning to its present-day use as a term of abuse directed solely at women, says, 'if such linguistic movements were to be charted comprehensively and in detail, we would have before us a map of the development of the double standard and the degradation of women.'(4) The myriad of abusive words that refer to women are well documented by both Greer and Faust. Faust says:

> In no other aspect of human life is there such a variety of terms having almost the same meaning; man's ingenuity knows no bounds when he wishes to insult *woman* (emphasis hers) and force her to see herself as he sees her (or as he wishes to think he sees her).(5)

In this respect, it is also significant to note that while men can insult us so fluently, the two most common terms of abuse directed at males are 'bastard' and 'son-of-a-bitch.' Neither of these insults is a reflection on the particular man himself, but on his mother, a woman.

Certainly the hordes of words with which men can put us down, and the drought of words with which we can return the favour, reflect the prevailing attitude toward women in our culture. So long as each new generation inherits and retains this imbalance, an anti-woman attitude can be maintained; insofar as every person learns of this imbalance, she or he can assume that the reason for it is the natural inferiority of women.

Faust notes:

> If she says no, she's a prude, a cold fish, a tease, a prig, a stiff-neck, or a professional virgin. If she says yes, she's a tramp, a slut, a whore, a piece, a lay or she's action or tail. (From being defined by her body, she is reduced further to being defined by a part of her body.) The last four terms, interestingly, are inter-changeably pejorative or complimentary, depending on the whim of the man.(6)

An example from an article by S.I. Hayakawa can make my point very well. The example refers to a fairly typical reaction upon meeting a Mr. Miller and learning that he is a Jew:

> If Mr. Miller is strange or foreign in his habits, that 'proves' that 'Jews don't assimilate.' If he is thoroughly American—i.e. indis-tinguishable from other natives—he is 'trying to pass himself off as one of us'. If Mr. Miller fails to give to charity, that is because 'Jews are tight;' if he gives generously, he is 'trying to buy his way into society.' If Mr. Miller lives in the Jewish section of town, that is because 'Jews are so clannish;' if he moves to a locality where there are no other Jews, that is because 'they try to horn in everywhere.' In short, Mr. Miller is automatically condemned, no matter who he is or what he does . . .
>
> If, as the result of our signal reaction we put ourselves on guard about our *money* immediately upon meeting Mr. Miller, we may offend a man from whom we might have profited financially, morally, or spiritually . . . that is, we shall act with complete inappropriateness to the *actual* situation at hand. Mr. Miller is not identical with our notion of 'Jew,' *whatever our notion* of *'Jew 'may be.* The 'Jew', created by intensional definition of the *word, simply is not there.* (Emphasis his.)(7)

We could substitute parts of this example. The mis-perceived person could be a Ms. Miller and her label is 'woman.' Upon meeting this person we might be struck foremost by her 'woman-ness' as Mr. Miller was seen fore-most as 'Jew'. All the stereotypic things we have heard about 'woman' might rush to the front of our brains—passive, a sex object, emotional, sweet, supplementary, etc.—and we could react with complete inappropriateness to the actual person. All the words we have that put down Jews can leave us with a particular attitude toward Jews. Likewise, the words we have that put down women can help solidify an attitude about women since we will see women only within that framework.

We have a number of words with which we define 'woman,' which nearly everyone learns, and which could conceivably influence a person's attitude toward all women. I certainly cannot enumerate all the words that categorize and stifle woman so that she is seen as a stereotypic thing rather than as the person she is. But I will cover many of the types of words that oppress in the last section of this paper.

Can Language Change Cause Attitude Change?

If you ask someone what they think language is, they would probably say something like, 'It's a tool to express our ideas to each other.' In addition to just expressing our ideas, however, language can help formulate them, as has just been discussed. This influence may be minimal or it may be extraordinary; we're not sure yet. But whatever the size of that influence, the next question is whether it is worth our trouble to try to change our language; whether changing the language could result in attitude change.

> After more than seventy-five years of attitude research, there is little, if any, consistent evidence supporting the hypothesis that knowledge of an individual's attitude toward some object will allow one to predict the way he (sic) will behave with respect to the object. Indeed, what little evidence there is to support any relationship between attitude and behaviour comes from studies showing that a person tends to bring his (sic) attitude into line with his (sic) behaviour rather than from studies demonstrating that behaviour is a function of attitude.(8)

In the field of attitude study, experiments have tended

to conclude that a person's attitude is no indication of how she or he will act. If an individual feels she or he is not sexist, that in no way guarantees that her or his actions will bear this out. We have probably all met a person who claims to be sympathetic to 'Women's Lib' but who in fact is unaware of his or her sexist actions. Joan Churchill was going to make a film in Paris at the same time Jane Fonda was to be in a film directed by Jean-Luc Godard. Churchill said, 'We are going to be Jane's back-up. She was scared to work with Godard. He's the worst kind of sexist—the kind who says he isn't one.'

It thus appears that the most efficient means to our end is to tackle sexist *actions* rather than sexist *attitudes*. Some studies, by Kelman, Cohen, Janis and King, and Lieberman, will serve to support the belief that behaviour change can cause attitude change.

Kelman had junior high school students write essays either in support of a type of comic book they liked or in support of a type they were against. The results showed that those supporting the initially disliked type of comic changed more in the direction favouring it than did those who wrote in support of the liked book, as measured by an attitude questionnaire before and after the essays were written.(10) Similar attitude change was found in a Yale study by Cohen in which students who were originally anti-police tended to change their attitude after writing pro-police essays.(11) Daryl Bem feels that when such behaviour change occurs, a person's '. . .new behaviour provides a source from which he (sic) draws a set of inferences about what he (sic) feels and believes.'(12)

Janis and King accomplished attitude change by role playing. They had college students present, as sincerely as possible, a speech from a prepared outline or else listen to such a speech. In all cases the position of the speech disagreed with the initial position of both speaker and listener. A questionnaire measured attitudes before and after the speeches and the scores indicated that the speech givers tended to show more opinion change toward the position of the speech than did the listeners.(13) Lieberman has also done a role-playing study where factory workers were advanced to higher positions. Their attitudes changed to fill their new roles. When they went back to being workers, their attitudes changed back to coincide with the behaviour required by the role.(14)

These studies do show a tendency to change one's attitude. The first three studies suggest that when verbal behaviour, or language, is changed so that originally disfavoured opinions are expressed, attitudes tend to conform. Cohen observed a possible explanation for this. He believed that when a person must express an opinion that differs from what she or he privately believes, the private opinions often change.(15)

Although the Lieberman study did not deal specifically with verbal change, it does indicate that attitudes change to coincide with behaviour. Another example is the behaviour change of large numbers of people necessitated by the school disegregation laws. In 1954 the decision came down from the Supreme Court that blacks should no longer be in mandatorily segregated schools. Attitudes toward school desegregation across the nation moved from 30% favourable in 1942 (before the laws) to 49% in 1956, to 62% in 1963. Even in the most hard-core areas of the South, approval of integration rose from 4% in 1956 to 28% in 1963.(16) Here is practical evidence that changing behaviour can affect attitudes.

The attitude research shows several things. First of all, it is fairly well established that *attitudes will change to conform to behaviour* rather than the other way around. Also, studies by Kelman, Janis and King, and Cohen indicate that changing specifically verbal behaviour can induce a change in attitude. And as witnessed by statistics of attitudes toward racial desegregation and Lieberman's observations, behaviour change aiding attitude change can work in very practical arenas.

Without being aware of the psychological principles involved, women have for many years been seeking behaviour change in many forms, assuming that attitudes will change thereafter.(17) Obviously, much more direct examinations are necessary. There should be a thorough examination of our language to determine what our words really communicate. There needs to be better understanding of the precise effects that language has on attitudes, perception and learning. And there should be more studies to see if language change can directly affect attitudes.

Words That Oppress
Armed with a general understanding of the relationship between attitudes and language, in what areas of our language are we presently aware that changes are desirable? The English language is replete with sexist words, phrases and connotations, words that are really put-downs, expressions that few people would use to refer to a black person but which are still socially acceptable to refer to women. It is helpful to break these down into several categories.

Debasing words
These are words that describe women in terms other than human, that is, as animal, vegetable, fruit, mineral, or any inanimate object. A few examples are peaches and cream, honey, sugar, a kitten, a sow, a prune, a pickle, a chick, a battle-axe, a pain, a doll, a dish, a nag, a pill, a dog or a bitch. There are many more.

Words that define woman by her sexuality
A quotation from Jean Faust earlier in this paper showed that women are often defined by their bodies and by parts of their bodies. Other favourites include a flirt, a hussy, a loose woman, twot or a once-a-month-bitch. Men

often project their own preoccupation with sex onto women and call them ball-busters, castrating bitches and man-eaters.

Words with sex-role value connotations

A large number of our words and phrases do not directly put down but their connotations do. Strength and weakness values are attached to words commonly considered masculine or feminine. Things childish and valueless connote femininity; things mature and important connote masculinity. Just the word 'manly' carries infinite unexpressed meanings along with it. Men insult each other by calling their brother, womanish, saying he runs like a girl, walks or talks like a girl, or worst of all, thinks like a girl. Even the word 'girl' puts us down. We're called girls until we're at least forty-five or even older. Boys become men sometime in their teens. Women are 'girls' forever, i.e., childish, incapable, in need of protection. Hurricanes, the Loch Ness Monster, and other disasters are feminine. Most of our first names are diminutives of the male form. Cars, ships, countries and other objects that men own are spoken of in the feminine. Lexicographer Ethel Strainchamps believes that, 'Emotive words acquire their connotations by reflecting the sentiments of the dominant group in a society . . .'(18)

Words indicating that woman is 'different'

Our language uses the noun 'man' and the pronoun 'he' in a generic sense, unless women are being specifically referred to. That is to say, that man is the standard, the normal and usual and that woman is the exception, the abnormal and unusual. 'Man' originally did refer to all human beings, but males appropriated it for themselves and came up with 'wif-mann' (now woman) for the rest of us.(19) 'Wif' means a female and 'man' means a human being. 'Man' is definitely not a generic term and has not been for a long, long time. Never the less, people continue to insist that it is understood that 'man' includes women too, while every woman knows in her heart that she in fact is not included, and wonders how long men would stand for having the shoe on the other foot: using 'woman' with it understood that it includes men too. As E. Merriam says, women are '. . . written about and spoken of either as non-men or a subheading under the main billing.'[20]

Likewise, words like businessman, chairman, serviceman, repairman, milkman and mailman reflect that these are male positions in which women are not welcome. At the 1972 Democratic National Convention many state delegates reporting their votes for the Vice-Presidency addressed the chair with 'Madam Chairman', a ridiculous contradiction.

Many suggestions have been put forth to correct the language's generically used pronoun 'he'. Neuter pronouns are a possible option. I know of a woman who used this new symbol when writing — s/he — but she doesn't know how to pronounce it. Some women use 'she' about 50% (or 51%!) of the time interchangeably with 'he'. Some use 'she' all the time except when referring specifically to a man. Others use the admittedly clumsy 'he and she', or better, 'she and he'.

Women are also seen as different and secondary by the '-ess,' '-x' and '-ette' endings on many nouns: actress, poetess, authoress, songstress, stewardess, suffragette, Jay-Cee-ette, usherette, aviatrix, mediatrix. The dictionary proclaims the meaning of '-ette' unabashedly as 'little,' 'female' or 'substitute'! If you can stand the insult, look up 'woman,' 'womanly,' 'female,' 'feminine,' 'Miss,' 'feminist,' 'gal,' etc. in a dictionary.

The word 'co-ed' expresses the male's attitude toward out right to an education. Education was masculine until males were forced to integrate it, make it co-educational. Education with just men is called education. Education with women is called co-education and we are the ancillary co-eds, the intruders.

The word 'woman' is often used as an adjective: lady umpire, woman scientist, girl Friday, woman lawyer, lady doctor, lady executive. All these show the unusualness of that situation and are qualifiers to indicate that women are different, and one must not confuse the lady doctor with just plain (male) doctor. When 'lady' is placed before a position or profession, it weakens it and lowers its status. However, when we use terms like 'male nurse' or 'male secretary,' somehow it gives the nursing and secretarial professions new class and a more serious stature.

Even the words we have for ourselves, *woman* and *female*, reflect otherness, different-ness from the standard man. The best solution I have heard for our language problem is to get a new language.(21) Until we do, however, we must be aware of how un-neutral our language is and aware of its influential effects. We can pay close attention to our own speech habits, encourage our friends to do the same, and continue to demand changes in the media, believing that as verbal behaviour changes, the attitude changes we desire will follow.

References

1 Ellis G. Ohlim, 'Maternal Language Styles and Cognitive Development of Children' in *Language and Poverty* edited by Frederick Williams, Markham Publ. Co., Chicago, 1970, p.219.

2 *Ibid.*, p.219.

3 Jean Faust, 'Words That Oppress' reprinted from *Women Speaking,* April 1970 by KNOW, Inc., Pittsburgh, p.1.

4 Germaine Greer, *The Female Eunuch*, McGraw-Hill, New York, 1970, p.279.

5 Faust, *op.cit.* p.1.

6 *Ibid.*, pp.1-2.

7 S.I. Hayakawa, 'The Little Man Who Wasn't There' in *Language . . . Man . . . Society; Readings in Communication* edited by Harold E. Briggs, Rinehart and Co., New York, 1949, p.132.

8 Martin Fishbein, 'Attitude and the Prediction of Behaviour' in *Readings in Attitude Theory and Measurement* edited by Martin

Fishbein, John Wiley & Sons, New York, 1967, p.447.

9 Sandra Lowell, 'Women in Film' in *Take One*, vol.3, no. 4., Unicorn Publ. Co., 1972, p. 45.

10 M. Rosenberg, C. Hovland, W. McGuire, R. Abelson, J. Brehm, *Attitude Organization and Change*, Yale University Press, New Haven, 1960. p.169.

11 Daryl J. Bem, *Beliefs, Attitudes and Human Affairs*, Brooks/Cole Publ. Co., Belmont, California, 1970, pp.55-56.

12 *Ibid.*, p.66.

13 Rosenberg, et.al., *op.cit.*, p.170.

14 Bem, *op.cit.*, p.66.

15 A. Cohen, 'Attitudinal Consequences of Induced Discrepancies Between Cognitions and Behavior' in *Public Opinion Quarterly*, vol. 24, 1970, p.297.

16 Bem. *op.cit.*, p.66.

17 Jean Leppaluoto, 'Attitude Change and Sex Discrimination: The Crunch Hypothesis' delivered to Western Psychological Association, Portland Oregon, 1972, p.1.

18 Ethyl Strainchamps, 'Our Sexist Language' in *Woman in Sexist Society* edited by Vivian Gornick and Betty Moran, New America Library inc., New York, 1971, p.352.

19 *Ibid.*, p.350.

20 Eve Merriam, *After Nora Slammed the Door*, World Publ. Co., Cleveland and New York, 1958, p.210.

21 Marilyn Farwell, 'Women and Language' delivered to a workshop: 'Women on the Move', University of Oregon, June 26, 1972.

Part Five

Racism

Introduction

In the colonial society, education is such that is serves the colonialists . . . In a regime of slavery, education was but one institution for forming slaves.
FRELIMO Department of Education and Culture, 1968.

Led by women, the fight for the liberation of women must be embraced by men as well. The battle for women's liberation is especially critical with respect to the effort to build an effective Black liberation movement. For there is no question about the fact that as a group, Black women constitute the most oppressed sector of society.
Angela Davis, *If they come in the morning . .*, Orbach & Chambers, 1971.

When I joined the factory, I never knew what a union was or a shop steward . . . they promoted me from grade A to grade B, but I found there was less in my pay packet. This is why we want to select our own shop stewards. We have so many grievances . . .
Mrs. Jayshree Doshi, Imperial Typewriters, Leicester, quoted in *The Black Worker in Britain* I.S./Chingari Pamphlet.

In his book, *How Europe Underdeveloped Africa,* Walter Rodney shows the connection between the slave trade, colonialism, and the development of capitalism in Europe.(1) Our present-day racialist society, as well as our psychological prejudices, stem from this historical period. This is not to say that racism is not directed against groups other than black people. Recent persecution of the Irish and the Jews is also inseparable from capitalist development.

This section concentrates on racial discrimination against blacks because this is its most extreme form now in our society, and this despite the immigration figures which show that two-thirds of the immigrants in this country are white—that there are more German immigrants than Pakistani.

A UNESCO publication on education in black independent Africa said:

> Of this population (of around 170 million), a little more than 25 million are of school age and of these nearly 13 million have no opportunity of going to school—and of the 'privileged' 12 million, less than half complete their primary education. Only three out of every 100 children see the inside of a secondary school while not even two of every thousand have a chance of receiving some sort of higher education in Africa itself. The overall estimated illiteracy rate of 80% to 85% is nearly twice that of the average world figure.
>
> Basil Davidson, in his *Africa in History*, explodes the myth of the Europeans bringing education to Africa: After forty years of British administration in Tanganyika, a population not far short of ten million people was able to enrol exactly 318 pupils in the class of standard 12 (the last in the four-year secondary course), while the number of school-certificates, permitting pupils to carry on with their studies, was 245.(2)

The expenditure on education in Uganda in 1959 was about £11 per African pupil, £38 per Indian, and £186 on each European child. In fact, as in this country in the nineteenth century, literacy was seen as a danger. The Beecher report on education in Kenya (produced in 1949) stated: 'Illiterates with the right attitude to manual employment are preferable to products of the schools who are not readily disposed to enter manual employment.'

In this country, discrimination is demonstrated by the fact that two out of five children in London ESN schools are black. Just as in the case of girls, a major form of oppression against black children lies in the whole ethos and culture of the school system. This is shown partly by the small number of black teachers in the schools, partly by the bias in school books about black people.

Look at these quotations from the Ladybird book on Africa:

'The Sudanese are very fine soldiers. They were raised and trained by the British.'

'The hotel (in Kampala) was staffed by cheerful, smiling Africans.'

'Lake Victoria was named after Queen Victoria by J.H. Speke, the Englishman who discovered it.'

'The farm workers (in Kenya) were Africans, who were very clever with the machinery.'

'Dr. Livingstone made friends with the Africans, who were all savages then, and taught Christianity.'

'Cecil Rhodes made peace with the African chiefs and used his fortune and his energy to develop the country. That is why it is called Rhodesia.'

'The Boers drove their ox-wagons far away into unknown parts of South Africa, inhabited only by savage tribes and wild animals.'

'Africa is growing up. People still believe in witch doctors and magic, and millions can't read or write. But they are eager for education. And in all the countries which were under British control they have been given their independence because they are able to manage their own affairs.'(3)

Or consider this writing found on the blackboard in a Liverpool school recently:

Very hot lands People are never so advanced or energetic as those in cool lands. They do not need to work so hard. Everything grows easily and they do not need a great deal of clothing.

Warm lands More civilised than the hot lands. White men have built many fine cities, roads, railways and have grown many useful crops.

Cool lands Here the restless, energetic White man lives. Summers warm, Winters cold. They need houses and plenty of food and clothing.(4)

Our very language discriminates against black people, as Bob Dixon points out at the beginning of his article. Martin Luther King confirms it:

Even semantics have conspired to make that which is black seem ugly and degrading. In Roget's Thesaurus there are some 120 synonyms for 'blackness' and at least 60 of them are offensive—such words as 'blot', 'soot', 'grime', 'devil', and 'foul'. There are some 134 synonyms for 'whiteness', and all are favourable, expressed in such words as 'purity', 'cleanliness', 'chastity' and 'innocence'. A white lie is better than a black lie. The most degenerate member of a family is the 'black sheep', not the 'white sheep'. Ossie Davis has suggested that maybe the English language should be 'reconstructed' so that teachers will not be forced to teach the Negro child 60 ways to despise himself and thereby perpetuate his false sense of inferiority and the white child 134 ways to adore himself and thereby perpetuate his false sense of superiority.(5)

In America, black slaves were forbidden their own language, their own history, even their own names in order to destroy their culture. Daniel P. Kunene illustrates how colonialism in Africa has carried out the same process. (cf. the schools in Johannesburg where history and maths had to be taught in Afrikaans.) Similarly, Rodney shows the contradictions between the content of colonial education and the reality of Africa:

On a hot afternoon in some tropical African school, a class of black shining faces would listen to their geography lesson on the seasons of the year—spring, summer, autumn and winter. They would learn about the Alps and the river Rhine but nothing about the Atlas mountains of North Africa or the river Zambezi. If those students were in a British colony, they would dutifully write that 'we defeated the Spanish armada in 1588'—at a time when Hawkins was stealing Africans and being knighted by Queen Elizabeth I for doing so. If they were in a French colony, they would learn that 'the Gauls, our ancestors, had blue eyes', and they would be convinced that 'Napoleon was our greatest general'—the same Napoleon who re-instituted slavery in the Caribbean island of Guadeloupe, and was only prevented from doing the same in Haiti because his forces were defeated by an even greater strategist and tactician, the African, Toussaint L'Ouverture.(6)

One way round the white cultural indoctrination now going on in our schools is to suggest programmes of Black Studies (e.g. NAME(7)) although Farrukh Dhondy discusses the limitations of this approach.(8) Again it must be stressed that changing children's books will not change a racist society; but it is part of the fight against such a society.

There are a number of publishers and organisations concerned with making available multi-cultural books and materials. (9)

References

1 Walter Rodney, *How Europe Underdeveloped Africa*, Bogle-L'Ouverture Publications, 1972.

2 Basil Davidson, *Africa in History*, Paladin, 1974.

3 D.S. Daniell, *Flight Five: Africa*, Ladybird, Wills & Hepworth, 1961.

4 *The Dragon's Teeth*, racism in children's books, plus catalogue of multicultural books, Merseyside Community Relations Council, 64 Mount Pleasant, Liverpool.

5 Martin Luther King, *Chaos or Community?*, Harper & Row 1968.

6 Walter Rodney, op.cit.

7 *Black Studies*, National Association for Multi-racial Education, K. Forge, 14 Thornton Road, Bromley, Kent.

8 Farrukh Dhondy, 'Black Kids Class Strife', *Radical Education* 2 1974/75

9 'Teaching about India, Bangla Desh and Pakistan', *Education and Community Relations*, October 73, Vol III No.9.
'Teaching about Africa', *Education and Community Relations*, March 74, Vol IV No.3.
'Education for a Multi-Cultural Society, a bibliography for teachers', *Community Relations Commission*, Russell Sq. House, Russell Sq., London W.C.1.
J. Elkin, *Books for the Multi-Racial Classroom*, Birmingham Public Libraries, 1971.
ed. J. Hill, 'Books for Children: The Homelands of Immigrant in Britain', *Institute of Race Relations*, 1971.
A. Day, 'The Library in the Multi-Racial Secondary School: A Caribbean Book List', *The School Librarian*, Vol.19, No.3, 1971.
Bogle-L'Ouverture Publications (Africa, The Americas, Caribbean)—141, Coldershaw Road, Ealing, London W13 9DU.
Progressive Books & Asian Arts (China)—624, Bristol Rd., Selly Oak, Birmingham B29 6BQ.
Independent Publishers (India), 38 Kennington Lane, London SE11 4LS.

New Beacon Books (Africa & W.Indies), 76 Stroud Green Road, Finsbury Park, London N.4.
Third World Publications, 67 College Road, Birmingham B13 9LR.

Three poems on racism
*Inderjit Randhawa**

1 I hate you — you faces pale
  You mask your feelings — drink too much ale
  Call yourself great — living on past glory
  You remember the victories but not the stories
  You have no feelings — you blue eyed babes
  You don't respect the living
  Only those in the graves
  I hope you never suffer
  The hate that I feel
  You may think I'm lying
  But I tell you this is real

2 I'm a pak, wog, a jew,
  I'm what I am
  So what you gonna do
  You gonna call me names
  Yeh tough guy
  You gonna blow me to bits
  Like Hitler did
  Sky high
  Then when we're all gone
  You gonna turn on your mothers
  Are the next to be your brothers?
  You can't get us all
  Oh no! Not you
  You can't get us
  But we'll get you

*A secondary school student

3 The writing on the wall
  I see it everywhere
  GO HOME WOGS
  And I say to myself
  I am going home
  One day

  School children chant
  As they walk past
  GO HOME WOGS
  How do they know
  The hurt that I feel
  How long it lasts
  How real

  The writing on the wall
  GO HOME WOGS
  Haunts me night and day
  Don't they know I'm just a cog
  Don't they know I long to do just what they say
  The writing on the wall
  I see it everywhere
  GO HOME WOGS
  And I say
  As I gulp
  And hold back the treacherous tears
  I am going home
  One day
  Do you hear.

All Things White and Beautiful*
Bob Dixon

A particularly strong aspect of the indoctrination carried on in children's literature is that of racialism. The present survey is intended, especially, for teachers who, in their daily work, are confronted with this problem. Firstly, we must consider the English language itself.

It still has to be brought to the conscious attention of most native speakers of the language that the word *black*, when not used in a purely literal sense, has overwhelmingly pejorative associations. Such usages are, for the most part, connected with: evil, as in *the black arts* and *black magic*; death, as in *the black death* and *the black flag*; disgrace, as in *black books, black marks, black list, black sheep, to blackball* and *to blacken*; and have criminal connotations, as in *blackmail* and *Black Maria*. Other associations, such as *black-leg, blackguard* and a *black look* merely add to the negative picture which is filled out by such phrases as *the nigger in the wood-pile*. In the context of contemporary Britain, a phrase like *to work like a black* might seem strange in view of the popular belief that black people live largely off the social services. The popular view on this point is contradicted by the facts. Words associated with blackness, such as *dark, pitch, shadow* and *night*, and phrases and idioms based on them, have similar connotations. With the word *white*, it is just the opposite. Although there are exceptions, the linguistic associations are overwhelmingly with goodness, beauty and purity. Most Indo-European languages seem to follow a similar pattern. In Czech and Russian, the words for *black* and *devil* are closely associated, etymologically, while further afield, certain aspects of this pattern of associations can be found, even

*Extract from *Catching Them Young* Vol.I, Pluto Press 1977.

in Chinese. The idea that such linguistic phenomena rose through the association of fear with the darkness of night before racial contacts had taken place on a large scale does not, of course, affect the thesis that real psychological damage is caused by this type of semi-conscious racialism built into everyday language.

Adult literature, as might be expected, is full of such figurative and symbolic usages—that is, where it is not openly racialist. Shylock and Fagin, Othello and Caliban all deserve a second look for there is no need for anyone to accept racialism in literature, not even if expressed in 'immortal' blank verse.

Children's literature, especially that intended for very small children, gives rise to particularly difficult problems as it more frequently operates on a symbolic and unconscious level. It is not possible to combat racialism instilled in this way by rational or conscious means as small children are not able to cope with the necessary abstract ideas. It is only possible to combat such racialism through literature for children which embodies civilized concepts carried at the same emotional and symbolic level. Here, however, it is necessary, first, to give some account of racialism in children's literature as it affects black people.

There are, clearly, different degrees of racialism to be found, some more vicious and destructive than others. It is at least arguable that the less apparent racialism is, the more psychologically damaging it can be. The fact that the more symbolic forms are usually intended for younger children may be an important part of the argument since such children are all the more impressionable. And when we speak of psychological destruction, it should be understood that racialism, in children's fiction as elsewhere, is harmful to all people, black or white, or whatever colour they may be, though, of course, non-white people obviously suffer from its effects far more.

The world of fiction for very small children often

includes recognisable elements from a child's everyday life. Naturally, it is important for a younger reader, as for any other, to be able to identify with what is being read. Thus, we can account for the prevalence of toys as characters in fiction for small children. Though bears figure largely in folk and fairy tales, it is the teddy bear as a traditional and very popular toy that must have given rise to the numerous fictional bears. The golliwog also started as a toy and now, it seems, no fictional *nursery* is complete without one. Essentially a golliwog is a doll with crudely stylized racial characteristics which are negroid in type. He belongs to the patronising and condescending racialism which includes coons and nigger minstrels. If we feel affection for him at all it is such as we might feel for a pet animal.

Enid Blyton, however, in the *Noddy* stories, gives the reader or the listener little opportunity to develop any such affection. Here, the golliwogs are invariably *naughty* and constitute a threat to Noddy, with whom the child is obviously meant to identify. The association of the golliwogs with fear and darkness is clearly seen in the following passage from *Here Comes Noddy Again*:

> Once in 'The Dark Dark Wood', Noddy becomes even more nervous.
> 'Where's this party of yours?' asked Noddy. 'I don't want to drive any deeper into the wood.'
> 'Well, stop just here, then,' said the golliwog, and Noddy stopped. Where was the party? And the band? Where were the lights, and happy voices?
> 'It's so quiet,' he said to the golliwog. 'Where *is* this party?'
> 'There isn't a party,' said the golliwog in a very nasty sort of voice. 'This is a trap, Noddy. We want your car for ourselves. Get out at once!'
> Noddy couldn't move an inch. He was so full of alarm that he couldn't say a word. A trap! Whose trap? And why did they want his car?
> Then things happened very quickly. Three black faces suddenly appeared in the light of the car's lamps, and three golliwogs came running to the car. In a trice they had hold of

poor Noddy and pulled him right out of his little car.

The golliwog who had come with him took the wheel, laughing loudly. 'What did I tell you?' he said. 'It isn't very good in the Dark Dark Wood! Hey, you others, there's room for one beside me and two sitting on the back of the car.'

'Wait a minute,' said one of the other golliwogs. 'This little driver has got some rather nice clothes on. We might as well have those, too!'

'Oooh yes,' said another golliwog. 'I'll have his lovely hat—it's got a jingle-bell at the top.'

'And I'll have his shirt and tie,' said a third golliwog. He pulled them off poor little Noddy. Then the driver leaned out and told the others to get him Noddy's dear little trousers and shoes.'

The black people, it should be noted, are taking Noddy's property from him.

'Soon Noddy had no clothes on at all. He wriggled and shouted and wailed. 'No, no, no! I want my hat, I want my shirt. You bad, wicked golliwogs! How dare you steal my things?'

But it wasn't a bit of good, What could the little nodding man do against four big strong golliwogs? Nothing at all.

The golliwogs piled into the little red and yellow car. Two were in front, two sat in the back of the car. One of them had Noddy's hat on. The moon shone down on it suddenly through the trees and Noddy wailed loudly.

'My dear little hat! Oh, do, do leave me that!'

'Ha, ha, ho, ho!' laughed the bad golliwogs and drove off at top speed. 'R-r-r-r-r-!' went the little car, and the sound grew fainter and fainter, till at last it couldn't be heard any more.

Noddy was all alone in the Dark Wood. He remembered the song of the golliwog. 'It isn't very good in the Dark Dark Wood,' and he stood up, trembling.

'Help!' he called. 'Oh, help, help, HELP! I'm little Noddy and I'm all alone and LOST!''

The child reader or listener, here, can be left with little doubt as to where his sympathies should lie. The emotionally loaded epithets applied to Noddy—*poor* and *poor little*—are even carried over to his possessions, his *dear little trousers and shoes*, his *dear little hat* and his *little red and yellow car*. The illustrations, in colour, strongly reinforce the emotional alignments indicated so clearly in the text. There is, for instance, a full-page picture of two villainous-looking golliwogs ripping the clothes off Noddy while the other two look on with broad smiles on their faces. The illustration following the extract just quoted shows a pathetic and frightened Noddy, naked in the dark wood. Retribution follows, of course, and the golliwogs are tracked down, tied up in a big sack and carried off to prison by the policeman.

It has to be emphasized, perhaps, that there is nothing inherently wrong in a black doll, as such. We need to centre our concern upon two factors. Firstly, as already touched upon, the golliwog is a racial caricature, of a negroid type. Since its first literary appearance in America, *The Adventures of Two Dutch Dolls and a Golliwog* by Bertha Upton, with illustrations by her sister Florence (1895), it has been remarkably standardized, both as a toy and as illustrations. It is interesting that Florence Upton was apparently inspired by a grotesque doll belonging to her grandmother. Secondly, we have to consider the role played by golliwogs in literature. As in the Noddy extract, they are normally cast in *naughty*, evil and menacing roles—that is, where they are not merely merry coons. Enid Blyton, in her simple way, and apart from the way in which she normally manipulated golliwogs in her stories, found their blackness a sufficient cause for dislike, as at the beginning of the first story in *The Three Golliwogs* (first published by George Newnes in 1944 and still available):

> There were once three little golliwogs who were most unhappy in the nursery cupboard. None of the other toys liked them, and nobody ever played with them, because their little mistress, Angela, didn't like their black faces.'

The three golliwogs in question here are called Golly, Woggie and Nigger, and nine of the eleven stories in the book are based upon mistaken identity as the three all look alike, of course. That's another irritating thing about black people in general.

The Epaminondas stories, by Constance Egan, are favourites of long standing, with an interesting history. The first appearance in written literature was in 1911 in *Stories to tell to Children* by Sara Cone Bryant. This included *Epaminondas and his Auntie* described as *A Negro nonsense tale from the Southern States of America*. Epaminondas is a type of the foolish or silly hero very common in folk literature but what is most important here is that the stories were taken over, expanded and developed by white people for the delectation largely of white children. Furthermore, unlike many simple 'heroes', Epaminondas does not triumph and the story may well represent, even in the original folk form, a *housing* (to use Paulo Freire's term) of the ideology of the oppressor in the oppressed, whereby the subject peoples come to believe in the inferiority attributed to them by their masters. The stories show a greater degree of realism, both in text and illustrations, than the Little Black Sambo stories but the hero is still of the simple type. In *Epaminondas Helps in the Garden*, Epaminondas's 'Mammy' plants some peas saying she hopes they'll come up quick and then goes off to take her eggs to the market leaving the little boy to look after things. She admonishes him not to let the hens get into the vegetable garden because if they do 'they'll have the peas up in no time.' Later, Epaminondas, growing rather confused, chases the hens into the garden in order to make the peas come up:

> 'Oh! Mammy,' he says when she returns, 'I thought the hens would help the peas to grow. I minded wot you said, Mammy, an' I was to take special care of them hens. An' I did, I drove them specially into the garden to help the peas come up quick . . .'

His Mammy calls him *just one foolish, foolish piccaninny*, but she relents at his tears and they kiss and make up.

Here we can recognise another type of racialism presented through the literary stereotypes of the coal-black mammy and the little piccaninny. The illustrations, by A.E. Kennedy, bear this out very strongly. The Mammy, who is very fat, wears a long blue and white dress with a large, white apron. On her head she wears a large scarf, dotted with red and tied at the front. Some kind of flat, red footwear completes the picture. Epaminondas is rather spindly, has short, red trousers, a red striped shirt and no shoes. Both are coal-black with big, rather round eyes and enormously thick, red lips (The hens are realistically drawn). An illustration towards the end of the story shows, in profile, the mother and son kissing. Their lips are so fat, however, that the rest of their faces are still about four to six inches apart. (In some editions, the illustrations are in black and white). Actually, a good deal of human warmth comes over in the story at the time Epaminondas's distress at his mistake and his reconcillation with his mother. It is a pity that it is presented in a format derived from the concept of the plantation nigger.

Interestingly, a group of infant teachers, conducting research into the influence of certain stories on their pupils, reported of the children's reaction to *Epaminondas and the Eggs* that 'They were ready to gloat as Epaminondas broke the eggs.' Perhaps these children, a few years later on in life, will become acquainted with the mischievous and ill-founded theories of Jensen, Eysenck and others which purport to show that negroes have *intelligence* inferior to whites. Of course, such psychologists assume that they know what *intelligence* is and, further, that what they take to be *intelligence* is of importance. It is rather a pity that Epaminondas, along with so many other fictional negroes, lends support to such theories.

The Black Penny by Alan Drake (University of London

Press, 1971) in racial terms, is the least explicit and overt of the examples we have been looking at. It could not be considered, I think, as one of the more harmful texts. As far as explicitness goes, in fact, this story is only one stage on from the basic racialism built into the English language which was noted at the outset of this study.

The story, for children of about eight years of age, tells of how David gets a new money-box. He says that all the coins he puts into it must be new and shiny, too, but one day he is given a very old penny which is almost black. Although he likes the penny and puts it into his box, it is not liked by the other coins:

> 'I ask you!' said the fivepenny coin and pulled a face. 'Black! Pooh!' . . . . . The fifty pence piece frowned very hard.
> 'I am not sure that he should be here at all,' he said, 'All of us are shiny and bright. He is dirty and black.'

When David and his parents go for a drive into the country, however, it is the black penny which saves them when the car breaks down. A water-plug has blown out and the old penny is just the size to fit into the plug hole. This enables the family to reach a garage. David says, of the black penny, *I am going to keep it for ever. I will polish it. It will look new and shiny.* His father, however, has the idea of gilding the old penny and, when this is done, the old penny has a very different reception from the other coins:

> 'They bowed. They all made room for the gold coin . . . . . .
> 'What a beautiful gold coat you have!' said the five-penny piece.
> 'You must be a very high person indeed.'

The old penny tells them:

> 'I am still that old, black, out-of-date penny underneath. I am sorry about that,' he said.
> But he did not look it.
> You and I know why.'

Yes, we know why he didn't look sorry about his change from black to gold. The pattern; the move from rejection, through a powerful visual change, to acceptance, is a familiar one. It is also worth noting that the idea of a test, a proving of worth, occurs in Enid Blyton's *The Little Black Doll*: Sambo has to prove his devotion to the pixie by braving the rain just as the black penny's worth is shown when the car breaks down. Each, in an emergency, was tried and found to be not wanting. After this initiation rite, they could move on to better lives. Here, the fact that the colour-change is mixed up with other elements such as the old-new component and the idea of status and hierarchy amongst the coins is merely incidental. It is worth remarking, too, that, in the original version of the story, there was no differentiation between the black penny and the other coins in terms of the old, and decimal currencies to obscure the issue. Racialism, in any case, is a part, though a very large one, of the concept of hierarchy which often seems, still, to be the basic framework of man's thinking, though it relates more to his less-than-human ancestry than to anything one might call civilised. It is remarkable how, twenty-three centuries later, *The Black Penny* should recall Plato's *Republic* and his men of gold, silver and of bronze.

Now it may be easier to comprehend the account an infant headmistress gave of a small West Indian girl who covered herself with white chalk and then announced proudly, *I'm a little white girl now*. Also, Bernard Coard's account,—in *How The West Indian Child is made Educationally Sub-normal in the British School System* (New Beacon Books, 1971)—of how black children portrayed themselves, and him, as white in their paintings and drawings, begins to be understandable. The attitudes and values expressed in the kind of literature we have been considering naturally lead to this kind of self-rejection. When such warped concepts are presented through the powerful medium of literature, and reinforced by the child's environment and through other media, not forgetting geography and history textbooks in school, it is not difficult to understand how such incidents happen. At the very least, the black child can, in the vast majority of cases, as far as literature is concerned, find nothing with which to identify, nothing which can relate him to a culture he can recognise as his own or a world he seems to belong to. Looking into literature, for such children, must be like looking into a mirror and either not seeing your face reflected back or, worse seeing a distorted mask.

Some people find difficulty in believing that very small children are race-conscious and since we have been considering dolls, some reference to sociological research making use of them may be instructive here. In the United States, where there is a long tradition of valuable research into the sociological and psychological aspects of racialism, the results of the first experiments involving children and dolls were published as long ago as 1947. Kenneth B. Clark and Mamie P. Clark in their article, *Racial Identification and Preference in Negro Children* report that they presented their 253 subjects with four dolls, identical in every respect save skin colour, and asked them to make a series of choices. The experimenters found that the majority of the children preferred the white doll and rejected the black one.

Some of the remarks the children made during the experiment are at once, funny, lovable and horrifying:

On the whole, the rejection of the brown doll and the preference for the white doll, when explained at all, were explained in rather simple, concrete terms: for white doll preference—'cause he's pretty' or 'cause he's white'; for rejection of the brown doll—'cause he's ugly' or 'cause it don't look pretty' or 'cause him black' or 'got black on him' . . . . .A northern five-year-old dark child felt compelled to explain his identification with the brown doll by making the following unsolicited statement: 'I burned my face and made it spoil.' A seven-year-old northern light child went to great pains to explain that he is actually white but: 'I look brown because I got a suntan in the summer.'

The children's words oddly strike through the detached, scientific prose of the study but their actions speak louder still:

> . . . . . . some of the children who were free and relaxed in the beginning of the experiment broke down and cried or became somewhat negativistic during the latter part when they were required to make self-identifications. Indeed, two children ran out of the testing room, inconsolable, convulsed in tears.

In case anyone should wonder what this has to do with the situation in present-day Britain, it can be reported that David Milner recently carried out similar experiments with dolls in Britain and his results confirmed, in considerable detail, the findings of the Clarks' study. David Milner worked with three groups of children: Asian, English and West Indian, and reported that, when the children were asked to say which doll they would *rather be,* 100 per cent of the English children, 82 per cent of the West Indians and 65 per cent of the Asians chose the white figure instead of, in the case of the black children, the relevant figure in terms of race. In fact, a great deal of research has been done on the foundations of racial attitudes in both black and white children in, for instance, South Africa, New Zealand, Mexico and Hong Kong. All the evidence seems to show that the patterns of racialism: the deprivation of cultural identity; the creation of self-rejection; the relegation to sub-human status—are everywhere and always the same.

I have felt it necessary to refer to the findings of these experiments because many people—and amongst them, depressingly, a great number of teachers—are reluctant to admit that racialist attitudes can be transmitted via literature. Faced with the kind of evidence we have drawn from children's literature, it is rather hard to contend that racialism is not actually present, though many people insist on being blind to it. Again, even when it is conceded that children's literature is often racialist, the point of view is often advanced that, nevertheless, this does not harm as it is, for the most part, at a sub-conscious or symbolical level. There can be little doubt that people can be influenced subconsciously—the evidence from subliminal advertising and research into learning during sleep would seem to confirm this. However, it seems reasonable to believe, quite simply, that we are influenced by whatever happens to us and that the more subconscious an influence is the more dangerous it can be.

We have been considering the child readers who are on the receiving end of the attitudes and values inherent in what authors write. It need not be supposed that the writers themselves are conscious of the values they hold. They would all, no doubt, be highly indignant at the charge of racialism. After all, very few people will admit to being racialists; it is usually at a subconscious level. An incident from my own personal experience brought this home very forcefully to me. I had been supervising a student on teaching practice and had been observing her work with a class of children of about eight years old. One particular English lesson involved the writing of accurate descriptions. The student had found six large pictures of faces and had set these up on the blackboard at the front of the class. Then she had asked the children to imagine that these were pictures of people wanted by the police. The children were to choose and to write a description so that the person could be identified. Although I wasn't particularly happy about this enlisting of the children in vigilante roles, I let that pass. What I was more concerned about was the fact that all the pictures were of black men. (The fact that they were all pictures of *men* is something I have only just realised but I don't wish to fight a battle over female sexism at the moment.) They were all pictures of *black* men. When I pointed this out to the student, she was amazed. Clearly, it had never occurred to her and she told me that she had merely leafed through copies of magazines and selected what she thought to be suitable pictures. Things being what they are, it is scarcely possible to believe that there could be an overwhelming preponderance of pictures of black people in magazines in question—rather the reverse. I pointed out that the children were being asked to associate criminality with blackness. (The fact that black people are usually disproportionately represented in prisons in mixed-race countries is an interesting, but different, question.) It is only fair to add that the student was very concerned when she realized the significance of what she had done and she did her best, in subsequent lessons, to bring about a better sense of values in the children's minds. This was not a student who wished ill to any child, white or black. She had simply, and unconsciously, absorbed the values of the society in which she had grown up and was in the process of transmitting them. The end of the story is also instructive. The student confided to me that she had discussed the matter, later, with other members of the staff. All, except one, thought that I had been making a fuss about nothing.

The charge of making a fuss about nothing is a familiar one to those concerned with values in children's literature. As far as racialism is concerned, the charge often appears in the more serious form of 'stirring it up'. These elements came out very strongly in the *Little Black Sambo* controversy of 1972 which began when Bridget Harris of the Teachers Against Racism group gave a statement on *Little Black Sambo* to 'The Times' which was to print an article on the new, boxed set of complete works of Helen Bannerman. The statement aroused a storm of fury from outraged readers who had loved *Little Black Sambo* when they were children and who thought that Teachers Against Racism were seeing harm where none existed. 'The Times' published at least twenty letters attacking the position outlined by Bridget Harris and only three in favour. It is interesting to correlate this ratio with the conclusion arrived at by E.J.B.Rose in *Colour and Citizenship*—that only seventeen per cent of the population are not racially prejudiced—though the letters might be seen, rather as more indicative of the readership of 'The Times'. More important is the fact that the three letters were all from black people. One of them was Dorothy Kuya, a community relations officer in Liverpool, who has done a great deal of valuable work in bringing about a conscious awareness of racialism in children's books. She wrote:

> The days have gone when the British could talk of Sambos, greasers, wogs, niggers and Chinks, and not find one of them behind him, refusing to accept his description and demanding to be treated with dignity.
>
> We now have to take note that we live in a multiracial society, and need to consider not whether the white children find LBS lovable, or the white teachers think it 'a good repetitive tale', but whether the black child and the teacher feel the same way.
>
> As a Black Briton, born and educated in this country, I detested LBS as much as I did the other textbooks which presented non-white people as living entirely in primitive conditions and having no culture. I did not relate to him, but the white children in my class identified me with him.

What is arresting is that so many writers of the other letters apparently found it sufficient to affirm that they, personally, had found the stories, or Little Black Sambo, charming, lovable, amusing, interesting or enjoyable. What is this supposed to prove? When I was young, a lad of my acquaintance enjoyed torturing frogs; some people have always derived sadistic pleasure out of inflicting pain on others; many find it amusing or interesting to throw stones through windows or set fire to forests. What does it all prove except that freedoms overlap and that some of us may have to forego some of our less socially acceptable pleasures?

Although there is little enough to choose from, fortunately it is possible to report that *some* positive attempts have been made within the field of children's literature to bring about a better state of affairs than the one we have been examining. It seems to me that they vary in the degree of success achieved and that, within the positive, as within the negative field, there are variations in ideological viewpoint. It is important to remember that the battle, especially as far as small children are concerned, must be conducted on a symbolical level which, in the broadest sense, simply means a literary level. After all, it is not possible to discuss the racialism of *The Little Black Doll* with a six-year-old, who would not be capable of the necessary generalized, abstract reasoning involved. One could provide concrete examples refuting the attitudes of such books but we need this in the medium of literature.

Judy and Jasmin by Jenefer R. Joseph (London, Constable Young Books, 1967) which is a story intended for children of about six years of age, is an attempt, although, I think, one based on a mistaken premise, to bring about a positive sense of values with regard to race. It provides, perhaps, the most obvious, if the lowest, starting-point for an examination of the more positive side. The story is of two small girls who are friends. Judy is, apparently, English, and Jasmin, Indian or Pakistani. The only indication of race comes at the very beginning where we are told that Judy had 'curly, fair hair' and that Jasmin had her hair in a 'long, straight, black plait', though the attractive illustrations show the two girls as of clearly different colours. We see a picture of the house where, semi-detached, they live side-by-side, we see them skipping together and we see them going to school with their mothers differentiated only, apart from their skin colour, by the colour of their raincoats and boots, though Jasmin's mother wears a sari and Judy's mother wears 'western' dress. At school they go into a tent and change dresses so that 'When they crawled out again, Judy was wearing Jasmin's yellow dress, and Jasmin was wearing Judy's red dress.' Further, when they lie down to rest 'after lunch', each takes the other's bed. Throughout the rest of the day, the other children get the two girls muddled and we are told that 'even their teacher wasn't sure which was Judy and which was Jasmin.' At the end, however, their mothers correctly claim their respective daughters and they all go home again. On one level, it is strange that the illustrations flatly contradict the story. No-one looking at the pictures could have any doubt as to the identity of the two children. On another level, it can be seen that this, in literary terms, is the equivalent of the integrationist attitude towards those groups who have immigrated to Britain since World War II. Jasmin's racial identity is completely ignored, in the face of all obvious evidence, and it should be noted, in the case of a racial group which has a very strong cultural identity of its own and which, unlike, for instance, the West Indians, whose original cultural identity has been largely destroyed, has resisted integration and cultural absorption. It may be better to be ignored than denigrated, as Sambo, the Little Black Doll, was but it is still not a solution.

Nor do the stories of Ezra Jack Keats, for children of about the same age, offer a solution, in racial terms, though they are well-intentioned and beautifully illustrated by the author. In such stories as *Snowy Day*, *Whistle for Willie* and *Goggles* (London, Penguin Books) there is certainly no attempt to pretend that the black children are white. They are black enough, but it is only skin deep. Nothing would be affected in Keats' stories if the characters were white. The whole, social, political and cultural significance of being black is left out. In fact, as Ray Anthony Shepard remarked in the United States publication, *Interracial Books for Children*, *Snowy Day* said that Black kids were human by presenting them as coloured white kids. The symbolic significance of the snow becomes apparent. The message seems to be that it is a white world but the black people can enter into it, integrate with it, with success and enjoyment. However, notwithstanding these reservations, it has to be remembered that the stories of Ezra Jack Keats represent a positive achievement, as is overwhelmingly obvious when they are compared with *Little Black Sambo,* the Epaminondas series and *The Little Black Doll.* Here is no simple little coon, no doll despised in his very blackness and nor is there any caricature either in words or pictures.

Elsewhere, too, in children's literature. it is heartening to note a raising of consciousness in the field of race relations. In *Journey to Mars* (Rupert Hart-Davis, 1969) one of the series of readers, *Adventures in Space,* the doctor on the rocket-ship is black, whereas, in stories about the adult world, black people are normally cast in menial roles—a point strongly reinforced in television advertising. In *Stumpy* by Clifford Carver (London, Oxford University Press, 1965) it is Perry, the black girl, who thinks of the plan for saving her white friend and herself when they are helplessly afloat on a raft in a strongly-flowing river.

It is *Stevie* by John Steptoe (London, Longman Young, 1970) however, which seems to me to succeed on every level. The story is meant for children of about nine years old but it operates at such a depth of human understanding that one wonders whether the term, *children's* literature, is really valid. Certainly, although the children in the story are black, and black Americans from the United States moreover, one would expect almost any child to be able to identify with Bobby (who tells the story in his own language) on a simple, human level.

Concerning the Colour of One's Skin
*Harry Sansum**

Mother: She's black
You hear?
I don't want her here
Just do what is right
And find one that's white.

Son: I can't,
I won't,
Don't say things like that,
DON'T.

Mother: Blacks is for blacks,
Not for my son,
What would the neighbours say
If you brought home one?

Son: Screw the neighbours,
And pardon me,
Screw your views too,
I go out with a girl,
Not the colour of her skin,
Or you.

Mother: It's just not the same,
It's not in the game,
Don't call 'em brother.
Think of the kids
Neither one or the other.

Son: Mum,
I love her.

*A secondary school student

Mother: You worry me sick,
Talking as you do.
I can't sleep,
I can't think,
Don't know what to do.
Why persist?
Resist
Find yourself a girl the same colour.

Son: You worry?
That's a joke,
You're selfish.
What will be will be,
Always thinking of yourself
Start thinking about me
You make my head ache
With your prejudice and pride,
Help me
Don't hinder me,
Face it and don't hide.

Mother: Leave her.

Son: No.
If she goes I won't get her back.
After all I'm not so white
And she's not so black.

African Vernacular Writing*
Daniel P. Kunene

When one thinks of the African writer in South Africa and Zambia, one thinks also of the missionary school through which he has obtained his education and of the establishment of such schools within the context of a christianizing mission. One asks oneself: if the missionary came primarily to christianize the African, what did he have to gain by making the African literate also? If even some of those overseas philanthropists who financed the mission asked this same question, failing to see why their hard-earned money, given to save souls, was being used partly to train teachers, the missionary on the spot, learning empirically from his day-to-day experiences, knew the answer. He knew that literacy—mother-tongue literacy, at any rate—was necessary for the obvious reason that, if he translated the Bible into the vernacular languages, he expected it to be read. Dr James Stewart, himself a missionary in South Africa, in the late nineteenth and early twentieth centuries, emphasized this point and added that: 'If missionary education communicated no other power than ability to read the Bible, it would still justify itself.'

The missionary on the spot, then, faced with the stark reality of his situation, saw in education a powerful ally, an instrument for ensuring the success of his primary purpose. Yet he gained much more than simply giving the people the Bible in their own vernacular. In those placed in his charge in school, he had a captive audience daily exposed to his relentless propaganda. So, for instance, by the time the children passed out of school, as young

*This is an extract from a paper which was read in a series of lectures organized by the Centre for African Studies, University of Zambia, in April 1969.

adults equipped to read the Bible in their own vernacular, they had already been told, in elementary school and beyond, things such as the following:

> In the olden days there was no peace among the black people. There were many wars. People attacked one another without provocation, they killed one another and captured each other's cattle.

and, about the days of the wars in Chaka:

> Truly, we who live today ought to thank God that we did not live in those days, but rather live in these days of peace, and of plenty, and of happiness.

Thus, and thus alone, can we begin to contextualize, and to get a deeper understanding of, identical sentiments expressed by some of our writers—we understand why Thomas Mofolo (1907), for example, describes the Africa of pre-missionary times as being: 'clothed in darkness, pitch black darkness, in which all things of darkness were done', and why he sees the Basotho as a debased, sinful and godless society out of which he makes his hero withdraw himself in disgust and go in search of a land of saints.

But since we shall be talking largely of attitudes, we might perhaps do well to go back and take a quick look at the beginnings of contact. The missionary, looked at in time perspective, must be regarded as a spiritual conqueror. Yet his conquest over the African followed a relatively long period of time in which his professed mission was viewed with suspicion, the new faith being sometimes totally rejected. But, understandably enough, as bringer of the means of ensuring continued survival *here on earth*, the missionary was most welcome. Stephano Andrea Mpashi tells us, in his *Abapatili bafika ku Babemba* (The missionaries come among the Bemba), that in 1894 Makasa, a chief at Mipini, extended his welcome to the first missionaries to come to his area; but that 'Though Makasa welcomed the missionaries, he had not the faintest idea what missionary work was all about . . . He welcomed them simply because he saw that they had guns . . . He thought they might help him if war should come.' The missionaries continued their overtures well into the following year. But when Makasa had eventually yielded to the slow persistent pressure from Father Dupont (nicknamed Motomoto by the Bemba), Chitimukulu angrily warned Makasa not to admit whitemen into his territory on pain of punishment. Father Dupont came to a rough welcome of arms-wielding warriors and human heads impaled on stakes. The hostility was summed up in the men's warning song to Motomoto and his party:

> You there, you there,
> We warn you to run.
> If you have no ears, if you have no ears,
> Your heads will not be on your necks tomorrow,
> But will grow on those poles over there.

Motomoto begged hospitality for the night, promising to depart the following morning. The next morning a woman with a wound came to ask for medicine from him, since the people had come to know that the white-man at Mwela had good medicines for treating wounds. Motomoto treated her, and the people were impressed. Motomoto was not slow to take advantage of this—he immediately sent a gift to the chief, who had also heard of his kind deed. Makasa changed his mind and asked Motomoto to stay.

Moshoeshoe, famous found of the Basotho nation and legendary lover of peace, actually sent out hundreds of cattle to *buy* himself a few missionaries, since he had heard that wherever they went they brought peace.

The African, then, accepted the missionary for practical considerations; the missionary, however, put a price on these—first, he used them to gain entry, and having done so, he made the African associate *all* these practical things with the Christian faith. Education was one of them.

In many cases the beginning of success for the missionary was the beginning also of serious tensions and divisions among previously unified and harmonious societies and communities—for the first time the terms *heathen* and *believer* were introduced into their vocabularies, and 'heathen' and 'believer' began to move into separate, hostile worlds across whose boundaries it was not uncommon for the words *heathen* and *believer* to be hurled back and forth in mutual abuse. Mission settlements to which the believers were herded by the missionaries in their separation of the *sheep* from the *goats* did not improve the situation. The important thing for our present purpose, however, is that the missionary, who was the bringer, not only of Christianity but also of literacy, succeeded in converting to his faith *some* of the people among whom he worked, even though there is much evidence to support Gann's statement that:

> It is open to doubt how far African religious ideas were funda-
> mentally changed by the new creed. It is true that the old gods
> did not resist the new God in open battle . . . The tribal gods,
> however, continued to wage a tenacious underground warfare.
> All too often Jesus or the Virgin Mary merely became additional
> spirits in the tribal pantheon (1958 pp.40-1).(1)

M. Xulu, a Zulu writer (1961?), tells it to us wherein he makes a Christian convert, who is also a local preacher —a man by the name of Dalisu, slaughter an ox as a sacrificial offering to the spirit of his recently deceased father (called in Zulu *ukubuyisa*—to bring back, i.e. to reincorporate the spirit of the dead into the community of the living, in particular into his immediate family). To his wife's fears that this will go contrary to their Christian faith, he suggests that they carry out his plan under the pretext of a family thanksgiving to God for a happy and prosperous year just past, and for the success of their daughter, Dora, in her teacher's certificate examinations. He admits that he finds it impossible not to mix his Christianity with an observance of his traditions which are in conflict with it, even though he would be ashamed to make his dilemma publicly known. S.E.K. Mqhayi (1943), Xhosa poet and novelist, tells it to us in a poem composed in praise of Christ, in which he calls Christ 'Senior of our Ancestors'.

The missionaries were not alone in modifying the thought patterns of the African, and in giving the writer his peculiar biases. They were only one section of a host of white comers who, by design or by accident, combined forces to remake the African in *some* image, usually their own image. The missionaries were greatly interested, and very much involved, in the creation of spheres of political influence in Africa. The more influence their own countries had, the more would the work of their missionary societies be facilitated. This is a very charitable view of the whole business, since it can be shown that some missionaries were involved for more mundane reasons than that. Therefore, when James Stewart says (1906, p.48), in adverse criticism of Mohammedanism, that:

> The religious and the political power of Mohammedanism are like two circles that largely overlap, and any reference to the causes influencing the religious progress of Mohammedanism requires occasional reference to matters of another kind.(2)

one wonders whether he continues thereafter to lay any claim to obejctivity. When the circles of the Christian religion and European political power overlap more and more, until, to all intents and purposes, they form one image, then the averment that the whiteman came to Africa with the Bible in one hand and the gun in the other is fully justified.

The gun was no less successful than the Bible, and the

physical conquest of the African, and his consequent political subjugation and economic exploitation were finally ensured, even though in many cases only after a long and determined resistance on the part of the African. Here again, the important thing for our present purpose is that this conquest finally did take place.

But, if we now concern ourselves with the eventualities of these historical process, and the relationships of inequality that flowed from them, we must yet pause a moment to state quite clearly that at first contact the African and the whiteman met on terms of complete equality. Our main concern is with attitudes, and what we have just said can be restated as follows: before conquest, both religious and military, the African welcomed the whiteman with the same hospitality that he would normally extend to his fellow African. And when the time came, he picked up his spear in defence of his land and liberty against the white aggressor with the same courage, conviction of moral justification, and determination to win, as he had done before when confronted with aggression by his black neighbour.

Nor did the African who dismissed the whiteman's religion mince his words in his condemnation of it. In 1884, *Uhadi waseluhlangeni* (Harp of the Nation), joining a controversy in the newspaper *Isigidimi sama Xhosa* (The Xhosa Courier), says:

> . . . We march to our very grave
> Encircled by a smiling Gospel.
> For, what is this Gospel?
> And what salvation?
> The shade of a fabulous *hili*(3)
> That we try to embrace in vain.

In other words the African was, at that time, not only physically free, but, more important, he was also mentally free. He saw himself as a man facing other men, even though their weapons might be more powerful than his. It was after conquest that attitudes began to crystallize and to harden. These are attitudes of growing confidence and self-assertion, to the point of being perpetually aggressive, on the part of the conquerors, and of corresponding diffidence and self-negation on the part of the corresponding admiration and even worshipping of the conqueror by the conquered . It is in this kind of situation that eventually the following questions become possible, and even claim respectability:

1 Is the European prepared to accept the 'native'? But never the reverse, *viz.* whether the 'native' is prepared to accept the European.
2 Is the 'native' ready to be accepted by the European. But never the reverse, *viz.* whether the European is ready to be accepted by the 'native'.
3 How can we blame the European for refusing to accept us if we behave like this? (Asked by the African himself.) A question the European never dreams of asking himself in reverse.

Writers with these types of questions lingering at the back of their minds will give you characters whose sole aim in life seems to be to evoke favourable comments and praise from the whiteman. We are given exactly that sort of creature by Henry Kadondo (1958) in his *Mtima wa Mfumu Kalanzi* (The heart of Chief Kalanzi); Kalanzi is made chief by popular acclaim after he kills a leopard that molests and sometimes even kills women on their way to the spring. He then establishes his own village. He takes all his problems to the District Commissioner at the *Boma,* and 'the Europeans' are always ready to come to the rescue with superior methods of combating all sorts of evils that threaten Kalanzi and his people. Among the appeals directed to the District Commissioner by Kalanzi are the following:

He requests the District Commissioner to have drinking wells sunk in his area. After inspecting the place, and seeing how hard it is on the people to have such little water, 'the D.C. shook his head and said 'I must do something' '.

Kalanzi writes to the D.C. to complain about the baboons, the wild pigs and the porcupines that devour his people's maize. The D.C. quickly dispatches game guards who destroy these pests.

Next, the Chief sends an SOS to the D.C. concerning a strange disease which has broken out among his people: 'without delay the doctors rushed to that place'.

Chief Kalanzi next writes to the D.C. to complain about the drought: *'Bwana,'* he implores, 'our eyes are raised to the heavens—when is the rain going to come?' The *Bwana* comes, but there is a limit to what even he can do, and we are not told that he brought any rain in the boot of his car!

Kalanzi is not only utterly dependent on the all-powerful 'Europeans', but is quite clearly flattered by their ready response to his numerous appeals, and more so by any priase that they bestow on him. For example: the D.C. thanked the Chief and said, 'Chief Kalanzi, you are a wise man and you take good care of your well . . .' Of all the wells in this area, 'yours is the best kept'. In this context we can well understand the statement that 'there were some (whether among Kalanzi's own people or among his neighbours is not at all clear) who were jealous of him because he was known to the Europeans'.

The people quite clearly not only fear the Europeans, but they indeed worship them: at a party at the *Boma* to which the people have been invited to celebrate the Queen's birthday, they are 'very surprised to see the D.C. eating with them'. Again: 'Because they feared the Europeans in the Provincial Administration, the area of Chief Kalanzi greatly improved.' The people wax eloquent in their admiration of 'the European's medicine'. After Kalanzi's death, they 'remembered his good work when he worked hand in hand with the government and the mission'. This situation produced 'Uncle Toms' by the thousand.

Perhaps this is as good a point as any to state the main thesis. It is done rather elaborately for purposes of clarity and emphasis:

1 In the colonial experience in Africa, not only has integration (in the broadest sense of the term) never taken place, but it was never intended nor contemplated. The tragedy of Africa, the basic problem that confronts us, is that of the contemptuous rejection of the African by the European. So Europe came to Africa and to varying degrees Europeanized Africa, but totally refused to be Africanized by Africa.

2 With the exception of a few individuals, *all* Europeans who came to Africa, for whatever purpose, were, in their relationship with the peoples of Africa, motivated basically by the attitude that the African *qua* African was an untouchable. As an African, he was fit for nothing more than cheap labour to be exploited for the enrichment of the whiteman and his motherland.

3 European attitudes to the African only begin to diverge at the symptom level. There are two distinct symptoms commonly known as segregation and integration, about which governments either stand or fall, but each of which may be traced right back to the basic cause, *viz.* the rejection of the African *qua* African.

(a) Those whom history has labelled as segregationists have said: He is not one of us, he never can be, he is happy, he is exploitable. We shall keep him socially separate from us, *and* physically as far as possible, even though we shall eat the food he has cooked and shall not object to his women acting as mother-substitutes for our children, etc., etc.

(b) He *can* be one of us, he *can* be our equal, says the other school. It is neither right nor fair, it is unchristian, to let him stay the way he is. We have to uplift him, we have to teach him to be like *us*, we have to teach him to be a *human being*. The closer he approximates to us (i.e. the more human he becomes), the readier we will be to associate with him socially—we might even increase his wages. This group has been labelled as integrationists or liberals.

There is a missing factor here, *viz,* a vital third group who are prepared to accept the African as they find him, so that the proximity of white and black would leave men as men, and let the resulting contact of cultures lead to what consequences they may. Only with this indispensable ingredient would true social and cultural integration be possible.

Our historians have either failed or refused to see that Cecil Rhodes' 'equality for all civilized men' and the nineteenth century South African Boer Republics' 'no equality in Church or State' arose from the same underlying motivating factor, *viz.* the rejection of the African *qua* African. Yet it is a situation which comes out very clearly and poignantly in the French and Portuguese colonial policies of assimilation. The handful of *assimilados* became an elite group among their own fellow Africans, and they could sit in the councils of Europe, but the unassimilated masses remained untouchable, fit only for cheap manual labour.

If some of our writers have character portrayals that describe their Ancestor-worshipping brothers as being for that reason evil and sinful; if, through their characters, they ridicule their own traditions and cultural values, and find everything infantile and ludicrous, it is because they, like those who exposed them to the propaganda of white superiority, are rejecting the African *qua* African. The only difference—the tragic difference—is that such writers are in fact rejecting themselves; and the irony—the tragic irony—is that they do so unwittingly.

As far as the whiteman is concerned, it is absolutely important that the blackman should be seen to aspire to be white, for this proves his (the whiteman's) alleged superiority and, correspondingly, the alleged inferiority of the blackman, and thus justifies the parent-child or protector-protégée relationship between the two respectively. If men aspire to godliness, it is because they have accepted the relationship between themselves and God that defines God as their father and them as God's children. There can be no question of mutual regard—God makes the laws, and man must either obey them or perish. This seeming aspiration towards the ideals of others creates a gigantic metaphor within which the aspirer is always measuring his worth in terms of the model. Thus the African is made an active participant in, and a contributor to, racist social structures.

References

1 L.H. Gann, *The Birth of a Plural Society,* Manchester University Press for the Rhodes-Livingstone Institute, Lusaka, 1958.
2 J. Stewart, *Dawn in the Dark Continent,* Oliphant, Anderson & Ferrier, 1906.
3 *Hili* — this term is used to describe a fabulous creature which sorcerors were supposed to be able to send on various errands of evil.

My Autobiography
*Phillip Christian**

I was born in Guadeloupe, one of the French colonies, in 1955. When I was two years old, my parents went back to Dominica, where me and my brother lived the childhood of our lives.

In 1967 my father came down the West Indies for Christmas and the following year he brought us to this country. When I came in this country I was eleven years old. In this eleven years in the West Indies, I can remember my first day at school. I hated it and wanted to go back indoors with my aunt. My auntie was our guardian because my mother and father were in England. Those eleven years in the West Indies I shall never forget. It's an experience I shall never forget because it has helped me to understand the way of life. I can remember a hurricane which was so bad that we had to stay indoors for a very long time. I can remember when the rain was hitting the roof and the house trembling, the force of thunder and wind, and me clutching my pillow and dreaming I was the master of the wind, rain, thunder and lightning, telling them what to do and bringing things back to normal again, and the people worshipping me wherever I go.

I suppose in everybody's childhood there is something, possibly a story or dream, of this kind, which now seems embarrassing if anybody hears it or gets to read about it, for this is how I now feel.

In happier times things were fine. I had a friend who is now my next of kin in the West Indies, his name is Chrispin with who I still keep in touch. His father is the

*A secondary school student

Chief Education Officer who grew up with my aunt. Though he belongs in a different class background, we remain still good friends.

Me and Chrispin did everything together. We had some chickens which we spent most of our leisure time fending for. We built the cage ourselves and his father gave us his permission to put the cage nearby his house. We also planted sugar cane which my father's acting guardian sold, fifty cents for four.

We had fantastic treks in the summer holidays. We once got lost and search parties came looking for us.

I can remember vaguely in my infant school a fat girl who always used to bully me in the playground, and me going home crying.

Anyway then at last the day dawned, it was time for me to leave the country I was brought up in. It was a Wednesday afternoon about four o'clock when we left Roseau, the capital of Dominica, where we had been waiting for hours. In waiting we sat by the quayside. There were also people who spent their Christmas there. There was a young boy about thirteen sitting in the harbour and he fell into the sea, and he couldn't swim, so my brother jumped in and swam with him to the shore.

The boat finally arrived and we got on and everybody waved goodbye. The journey on the boat was very nice, meeting people that you did not know back home. Anyway we arrived in England on the seventh of February in Southampton where my mother was waiting for us. The day we arrived I recall was very cold so that my mother had to go out and buy cardigans because we never had any in the West Indies.

The years passed so quickly that I can't hardly remember anything up to this day. Well, there's my mother who doesn't look her age, she is not as good as my aunt back home. I suppose I feel this way because I spent most of my childhood away from her. My mother is a very strict person who abides by the rules and regulations. Now at the age of seventeen I don't really know how much love I have got for her, as my aunt back home, reason mentioned above. My mother you don't really know when to approach her with anything because she is sometimes in a good humour and sometimes she is not.

I can remember it was about three weeks after arriving in this country I went to Plashet park with my younger brother. On our way out, outside the gates, a group of about four boys called me a black bastard. I got so mad that I jumped on them. I beat them up and afterwards I was sorry. But nowadays if anybody calls me names I just say I am black and I am proud of it. I have experienced that that's the best way to beat this so called Racial Discrimination.

Part Six

Class and the Classroom

Introduction

The whole history of mankind (since the dissolution of primitive society, holding land in common ownership) has been a history of class struggles, contests between exploiting and exploited, ruling and oppressed classes.
Karl Marx & Friedrich Engels, *Manifesto of the Communist Party*, 1848.

Political education goes together with literacy training. OMA, Organisation of Angolan Women (women's arm of the MPLA), quoted in *Spare Rib* No.26, July 1974.

The party's fundamental task in relation to literature and culture is raising the level of literacy—simple literacy, political literacy, scientific literacy—of the working masses, and thereby laying the foundation for a new art.
Leon Trotsky, *Class and Art*, 1924.

An important difference between the categories of sex and race and that of social class is mobility. Black and female remain black and female, but you can change your social class.

80% of Asian students studying in the USA stay there after the completion of their studies.[1] Similarly, most working class students who succeed in the educational system are absorbed into the middle classes and reject their class background (see Quintin Hoare's article which also refers to the class background of teachers). This presents an obvious dilemma to the socialist teacher who is teaching working class children.

One solution is what Trotsky calls 'political literacy.'[2] Politics, however, is the one thing that you are not supposed to teach in a committed way in our schools. Religion is compulsory, but politics outlawed. Certainly, literacy is rarely seen as a political activity; rather it is considered to be a neutral *technical* process. But it has already been shown in the previous two sections of the book that literature is saturated with political bias in the form of sexism and racism. In the same way class bias is obvious: in the way history is usually taught in school; in the social environment presented in Ladybird books (3); and in what Harold Rosen calls the 'language of secondary education'(4).

Aiming at impartiality is no way to combat this, because impartiality is impossible. In the words on the front cover of *The Plebs*: 'I can promise to be candid but not impartial.' Or as Rosen says: 'It is becoming increasingly difficult to refuse to take sides.'

However, the reality of teaching in a school complicates the problem of distinguishing which side is which. By most pupils' definition (particularly in the secondary school), the teacher is already on one side—the other side from the pupils, the side of power and authority. It is no easy matter to change sides, given the pressure on teachers of workload, class size, lack of accommodation and equipment. Besides, as a teacher you don't want to change sides completely, because part of the struggle is uniting with other teachers in the union (as well as supporting student demands.)

Changing the curriculum and fighting through the union may almost appear simple courses of action when compared with the problem of pedagogy. How do you combine socialist education with encouraging students to initiate learning and action *themselves?* This is the issue facing the English teachers at Langdon Park School in Poplar who recently taught a course on the theme 'Stories from Local History', and published the resulting children's work in a booklet called *The People Marching On.*(5) Or again, the main criticism (in *Women's Report*) of Chris Searle's book, *Classrooms of Resistance,* was that *his* voice was coming through too strongly in the pupils' writing.(6)

Ken Worpole's article stresses the importance of a 'local, democratic process of book-production' as the alternative to commercial publishers. In school this can mean that 'the language and syntax used in the books is precisely that used by the children themselves: their key words rather than ours.' (This is Paulo Freire's idea, and a variation of it has been adopted in Tanzania where the rate of illiteracy is over 80% among men and over 90% among women. Traditional stories are being taped, transcribed and translated into Kiswahili to provide adult reading materials.)(7) The children must become authors. The teacher's role is to 'locate their audience, and make available to them the means of production.'

It is precisely the tension between this pedagogical aim and the aim of a socialist curriculum which has to be worked at and resolved.

References

1 Keith Buchanan, 'The Geography of Empire', *Spokesman*, August, 1971.
2 Leon Trotsky, *Class and Art*, 1924.
3 Ken Worpole, 'Ladybird Life,' *New Society*, 23rd December 1971.
4 ed. Douglas Barnes, *Language, the Learner and the School*, Penguin 1969.
5 *The People Marching On*, Langdon Park School (Annexe), Limehouse, London E.14. 1976.
6 *Women's Report*, Vol. Issue 1, Nov/Dec 1975.
7 Simoni Malya, 'Traditional Oral Literature for Post-Literacy Reading Materials,' *Prospects* Vol VI, No.1, 1976.

The Plum Tree
Bertolt Brecht

In the yard stands a small plum tree
Though you'd hardly believe it was one.
It has a railing round it
So no-one can knock it over.

It can't grow any bigger
Though that's what it wants to do.
That's out of the question —
It gets too little sun.

You'd hardly believe it was a plum tree
For it never bears a plum.
But it is a plum tree
You can tell by the leaves.

Cultural Deprivation and Compensatory Education
Martin Hoyles

The term 'cultural deprivation' was first used in America in the 1950s. This was in connection with 'compensatory education' schemes such as the Higher Horizons Program (1956-62), and later the pre-school Operation Head Start (1964). Culture was defined as middle-class or 'high' culture. It was obviously not being used in the anthropologist's sense of the word. (Otherwise, of course, a title such as 'The Culturally Deprived Child' would have been meaningless.)[1] The theory behind such programmes was basically psychological: at that time the New York City school system employed more than a hundred psychologists and no sociologists.[2] Terms were used, such as 'cage-reared and pet-reared rats and dogs', to describe different types of children; and there was a stress on the life-long importance of experience during the first four years of life.

The theory became popular and was widely accepted, partly because it appealed in different ways to separate political ideologies. Liberals saw it as an attempt to be more egalitarian, providing equality of opportunity, developing potential talent, helping the underprivileged. They also thought of it as a way of combating racism by emphasising the social nature of intelligence as against genetic theories. Conservatives, on the other hand, saw it as a means of social control, preventing discontent and riots (e.g. by the Los Angeles blacks in 1965), avoiding economic wastage, and imbuing middle class virtues.

Either way, what is common to both is the 'vacuum ideology' which views certain children as deficit systems—a social pathology model. So Mrs Lyndon Johnson can say: 'Project Head Start is the most exciting, productive and practical project any government can embark on. It will be the effort of volunteers and professionals throughout this country to reach out to one million young children, lost in a gray world of poverty and neglect, and lead them into the human family. Circumstance has stranded them on an island of nothingness.'(3)

On this 'island of nothingness' are stranded the racial minorities too: 'The Negro is only an American and nothing else, he has no values and culture to guard and protect.'(4) Similarly, an educator is quoted as saying: 'Indian children have no home experience in art or music'; and an official: 'We must go back to the (Indian) home to find the lack of patterns that should have been learned.'(5)

It is the home and family which are considered the most pernicious influence in perpetuating this 'gray world'. Inadequate mothering, mothers who do not talk to their children, mothers who go out to work, separated parents, lack of books in the house, absence of a stimulating environment:

> Visually, the urban slum and the over-crowded apartments offer the child a minimal range of stimuli. There are usually few if any pictures on the wall, and the objects in the household, be they toys, furniture or utensils, tend to be sparse, repetitious and lacking in form and colour variations. The sparsity of objects and the lack of diversity of home artefacts which are available and meaningful to the child, in addition to the availability of individualised training, give the child few opportunities to manipulate and organise and discriminate the nuances of that environment.(6)

Educational Administrators explain the problems of educating the Sioux Indian reservation child:

> The school got this child from a conservative home, brought up speaking the Indian language and all he knows is grandma. His home has no books, no magazines, radio, television, newspapers: it's empty! He comes into school and we have to teach him everything. The Indian child has such a meagre experience. When he encounters words like 'elevator' or 'escalator' in his reading he has no idea what they mean.(7)

A language deficit is also thought to exist in these deprived children: 'From what is known about verbal communication in lower-class homes, it would appear that the cognitive uses of language are severely restricted . . . What is lacking . . . is the use of language to explain, to describe, to instruct, to inquire, to hypothesize, to analyse, to compare, to deduce, and to test. And these are the uses that are necessary for academic success.' Consequently an 'academically oriented' pre-school programme has been devised to teach poor children language skills.(8)

In this country, the ideology of cultural deprivation has been adopted by a number of educational reports. The Plowden Report says that 'the schools must supply a compensating environment', and it advocates positive discrimination in favour of deprived schools.(9) The Newsom Report was written specifically about the deprived, and maintains that discussions in school may 'begin to reveal, even at a very modest level of understanding, how aspects of government and economics and social justice touch us all and that society is not simply divided into Us and Them.'(10) In the same way, the Schools Council Working Paper 27, *Cross'd with adversity*, is full of middle-class cultural assumptions. The writers of this pamphlet are quite clear as to which is the deprived culture and how to remedy it: 'It may have virtues of its own, but the warmth and intensity of social life in a Coronation Street, transcended only by television, the Press and the conventional aspects of pop culture, is simply no substitute for the wider horizons of travel, of aesthetic interests, and of interaction with other social groups.'(11)

In America, the compensatory education programmes did not produce the results intended. There were some short term improvements; but these disappeared after a few years. (A similar conclusion has been reached regarding the 'Educational Priority Area Project' carried out recently in this country.)[12] Two theories were subsequently put forward to account for their failure. One blamed the vicious circle of poverty which guarantees a self-perpetuating and ineradicable culture of poverty. The damage was done early in a child's life and so was irreparable: 'By the age of six or seven slum children have absorbed the basic values of the subculture and are not psychologically geared to take full advantage of changing conditions or increased opportunities.'[13] The other was a reversion to biological theories. Compensatory education had failed because genetic factors prevail over environmental ones in accounting for I.Q.; and those environmental factors which do affect intelligence occur pre-natally and in the first year of life, associated mainly with the nourishment of the mother and child.[14]

All this, so far, has been within the context of agreeing with the premises on which the concepts of cultural deprivation and compensatory education are based. Basil Bernstein's work provides a link between those who support these premises and those who oppose them. His theory of language codes has been used in America to support compensatory education programmes, but Bernstein has since criticised the concept of compensatory education and has insisted that he makes no value-judgement on the different codes.[15]

This issue of value judgement has been one of the main starting-points of the opposition. The idea of 'the subculture of poverty as the zero-point on a continuum which leads to the working-class and the middle-class'[16] is rejected, and the anthropologist's 'value-free' approach to culture is assumed. It is significant that the anthology of essays, *The Culture of Poverty: A Critique*, originated from the 1966 meetings of the American Anthropological Association.[17]

This approach leads to a *difference* theory rather than a *deficit* theory;[18] but before the differences are examined, the similarities are pointed out.

In the sphere of language, William Labov's research indicates that the syntactic structures of Black American speech and Standard English are basically the same: 'The concept of verbal deprivation has no basis in social reality. In fact, Negro children in the urban ghettos receive a great deal of verbal stimulation, hear more well-formed sentences than middle-class children, and participate fully in a highly verbal culture. They have the same basic vocabulary, possess the same capacity for conceptual learning, and use the same logic as anyone else who learns to speak and understand English.'(19)

The deprived home is questioned: what is a good home? what are pre-school educational experiences? what is an orderly stimulating home environment?—'We should also remember . . that we have no description of the home life of the pupils said to be handicapped which would justify the assertions made . . . Nor is it clear why the play with broomsticks and kitchen pots of these children should be inferior to that of 'middle-class' children, whose play with household objects is often encouraged in colour supplements and progressive child-rearing manuals as 'imaginative' and 'resourceful'.'(20)

The notion of basic differences in intellectual development is also challenged: 'Poor children's intellect shows healthy development because these children are active learners who play a major role in shaping their own growth,' and 'their environment is quite adequate for promoting the basic forms of cognitive activity.'(21) This position is supported by a study of the Puluwat Islanders. They score very badly on I.Q. tests and could be described as unintelligent and incapable of abstract thought, yet they possess an extensive body of navigational knowledge which operates at a high level of abstraction: 'There is reason to suspect the validity of the one distinction upon which there is now considerable agreement, that between middle-class abstract and lower-class concrete thinking.'(22)

The reason why these similarities are viewed as differences, it is argued, is that they are being viewed from the outside. One culture is researching another culture without really understanding it. Often the observation is of a very narrow behavioural range, and the 'deprived' are compared not necessarily with middle-class reality but with middle-class ideals. Also statistics are misused (e.g. on mental illness, matriarchal families, illegitimacy), and there is a concentration on the demoralised, addicted and delinquent.(23) A truncated view of the whole is presented and there is an assumption of homegeneity, whereas there can be a variety of response to the same situation, as well as internal inconsistency.

Nevertheless, certain differences are admitted, but they are not seen as being inferior. These are differences of history, culture, life-style, ways of using language. They only become disadvantages when there is culture-conflict —when they come up against a more powerful culture. This, it is maintained, is what happens when children from racial minorities or the lower classes go to school. A study of Cherokee reservation schools suggests that from the first the Indian child may experience school as alienatory. Reservation schools are organised spatially and temporally in ways taken for granted by the white teachers, but not integral to Indial social arrangements. Similarly, teachers offend the Indian sharing-ethic by requiring Indian pupils to work in competition with each other.(24)

Teachers in slum schools discriminate against certain children:

> Thus, before these youngsters have completed a full four months of schooling, their educational futures have been 'tracked' . . . Some youngsters are selected very early for success, others written off as slow. Because differential teaching occurs and helps to widen the gap between children, the opportunity to move from one category to another is

limited. In addition, the children too become aware of the labels placed upon them. And their pattern for achievement in later years is influenced by their feelings of success or failure in early school experiences.(25)

So the proponents of the theory of cultural deprivation and their opponents have set themselves different tasks: 'Operation Head Start is designed to repair the child, rather than the school; to the extent that it is based upon this inverted logic, it is bound to fail.'(26) There seems to be a consensus among the opponents that it is the school, not the home, which is to blame: 'Not only is compensatory education a failure, but it also tends to divert attention from the real issue, namely reform of the public schools.'(27) Norman Friedman sees the theory being used to cover up the educational ineffectiveness of teachers and schools. He blames segregated schools—not black culture.(28)

This lands the opponents in a paradoxical position. If different cultures are of equal worth and value, what should the schools be doing? The answer comes that they should be designed for a polycultural input. But what about the output?—'Education for culturally different children should not attempt to destroy functionally viable processes of the sub-culture, but rather should use these processes to teach additional cultural forms. The goal of such education should be to produce a bicultural child who is capable of functioning in his sub-culture and in the mainstream.'(29) In other words the aim is still the same: to enter mainstream culture, which, if it means high culture, is ironically a minority culture. Simply, the process has become more subtle. Each child is seen as having his own culture which must be respected, but it is not suggested that middle-class children be initiated into working-class culture, or whites into black culture!

Another weakness with the 'cultural neutrality' position is its tendency to treat the conditions of material poverty as irrelevant. It has been said that we should change poverty—not the culture of the poor. But if the culture of the poor is of equal worth, then why bother to change poverty? We end up with a 'noble savage' idea of the poor.

The major criticism, however, of the opponents' position is that it lacks any historical, social analysis. The terms used are uncritically adopted from those who support the theory of cultural deprivation: the poor, ethnic minorities, the lower classes. But who are the lower classes and what is meant by poverty? How poor do you have to be to be poor? What is the cut-off point? Who decides where it is? The working class is rarely, if ever, mentioned; it is always minorities—groups which are somehow regarded as natural entities. Consequently, when mainstream culture is referred to, it is assumed that this is majority culture. The point is that you cannot have a theory about poverty without it containing a theory about wealth, so you cannot theorize about the working class without a theory of capitalism, because the two are interdependent.

The error lies in a basically anthropological perspective which tends to isolate cultures, rather than showing their interdependence and the power relations between them. Where it does look at culture-conflict, it concentrates on the school. Other points of contact are ignored. Occasional references are made to the necessity of changing society in order to change the schools, but they are as vague as that. No analysis is made of the causes of the situation which has to be changed, or how it could be changed.

The opponents attack the social pathology model of social class, maintaining that the racial minorities, the lower classes and the poor are not 'sick' as compared with the healthy, white middle class, but that their cultures are of equal value. This position ends up defending the healthy nature of all classes in society. If, on the other hand, one stresses not the equal value but the equal alienation of all sections of society, one ends up in a quite different position. A social pathology model of a particular class can then be replaced by a pathology model of the whole *class* system. As Annie Stein says, 'The role of the 'honest' social scientist must be to begin the systematic study of the pathology, not of the ghetto, but of the oppressing society.'(30)

References

1 Frank Riessman, *The Culturally Deprived Child*, Harper & Row 1962.
2 Norman L. Friedman, 'Cultural Deprivation,' *Journal of Educational Thought*, Vol. 1 No. 2 August 1967.
3 quoted by Annie Stein, 'Strategies for Failure', *Harvard Educational Review*, Vol. 41 No. 2 May 1971.
4 quoted by Stephen Baratz & Joan Baratz, 'Early Childhood Intervention', *Harvard Educational Review* Vol. 40 No. 1 Winter 1970.
5 quoted by M.L. Wax & R.H. Wax, 'Cultural Deprivation as an Educational Ideology,' in ed. Eleanor Burke, *The Culture of Poverty: A Critique*, Simon & Schuster 1971.
6 Martin Deutsch, 'The Disadvantaged Child and the Learning Process', in.ed.
   A.H. Passow, *Education in Depressed Areas*, Teachers College Press 1963.
7 M.L. Wax & R.H. Wax, 'Formal Education in an Indian Community,' *Social Problems Monograph* II Spring 1964.
8 Carl Bereiter & Siegfried Engelmann, *Teaching Disadvantaged Children in the Pre-School*, Prentice-Hall 1966.
9 The Plowden Report, Children and their Primary Schools HMSO 1967.
10 The Newsom Report, Half Our Future, HMSO 1963.
11 'Cross'd with adversity', *Schools Council Working Paper 27*, Evans/Methuen 1969.
12 Philip Robinson, *Education and Poverty*, Methuen 1976.
13 Oscar Lewis, 'The Culture of Poverty', *Scientific American* Vol. 215 No. 4 October 1966.
14 Arthur R. Jensen, 'How much can we boost I.Q. and scholastic achievement?,' *Harvard Educational Review* Vol. 30, No. 1 Winter 1969.

15 Basil Bernstein, 'A Critique of the Concept of 'Compensatory Education?',' in ed.
   David Rubenstein & Colin Stoneman, *Education for Democracy*, Penguin 1970.
16 Oscar Lewis, op.cit.
17 ed. Eleanor Burke Leacock, op.cit.
18 Frederick Williams, 'Some Preliminaries and Prospects,' in *Language and Poverty*, Markham Pub. Co. 1969.
19 William Labov, 'The Logic of Nonstandard English,' in ed.
   Nell Keddie, *Tinker, Tailor. . .*, Penguin 1973.
20 'Ideological Use of the Cultural Deprivation Concept,' in *Sorting Them Out*, Open University 1972.
21 Herbert Ginsburg, *The Myth of the Deprived Child*. Prentice-Hall 1972.
22 Thomas Gladwin, *East is a Big Bird*, Harvard University Press 1970.
23 Eleanor Burke Leacock, op.cit.
24 R.V. Dumont, & M.L. Wax, 'Cherokee school society and the inter-cultural classroom,' in *School and Society*, Open University 1971.
25 Estelle Fuchs, 'How Teachers Learn to Help Children Fail,' in.ed.
   Nell Keddie, op.cit.
26 William Labov, op.cit.
27 Herbert Ginsburg, op.cit.
28 Norman L. Friedman, op.cit.
29 Stephen Baratz, & Joan Baratz, op.cit.
30 Annie Stein, op.cit.

Well, I mean, he had the chance didn't he?
*Craig Paice**

Elsie sits with her curlers in
Putting out her cigarette in the greasy tea which slops
Around the soggy biscuit in the cheap and chipped saucer

'Billy'
She shouts.
(she's reading the paper
digging her ear
adjusting her straps
slicking the ash
[whose powdered waste drifts and glides down
into the dog's water bowl])
'You're not sitting down here like that
Go and wash your hands.'

Albert comes,
Pushing Billy as he makes his weary exodus
and playing a rasping tune on his chin-stubble
he scrapes the sweat from under his arm
so it mingles with the dirt in his fingernails.
Sitting down he complains
'That boy is like a dust-bin
I don't know who he gets it from.'

As Billy washes the soap to wash himself
He remembers that today is his big day. Today Billy is
going to the Youth Employment Office where he will be
offered all kinds of good jobs and worthwhile employment for a growing lad of fifteen at secondary modern

*A secondary school student

school. You know the sort, electrician's mate, butcher boy, plumber's assistant. All good stuff. It's not so much the lack of interesting jobs that's bad as the gnawing feeling of why he's in the position he's in. It's not his fault is it?

Meanwhile . . . .

Way down yonder, in Woodford Green
Daddy mixes drinks for the social machine
Which turns so properly, just how it's done
'Gin, Cynthia, darling, oh do have some.'

'Where's Anthony,' says Mummy, 'Where IS that boy?'
'I did so want him to meet Julie and Roy'
'Oh here's the car now, quiet everyone,
This is Anthony—our son.'

Oh hasn't he grown said the crowd with a roar
As they showered him with hand shakes smiles and more,
'Just like his father,' one's heard to say,
'No, more like his mother,' 'No, surely not,' 'Nay.'

Anthony 'work makes me puffy' Rand
(He's shaken Reginald Maudling's hand)
He's been to Eton, he's been to France
Tonight he's been to another deb's dance.

He's got no need for Y.E. O.'s
He can live how he wants till the money goes,
And that isn't likely so he's all right
What about Billy?

Beyond the Classroom Walls
Ken Worpole

He [the writer] should never say to himself, 'Bah! I'll be lucky if I have three thousand readers', but rather, 'What would happen if everybody read what I wrote?' He remembers what Mosca said beside the coach which carried Fabrizo and Sanseverina away, 'If the word love comes up between them, I'm lost'. He knows that he is the man who names what has not yet been named or what dares not tell its name. He knows that he makes the word 'love' and the word 'hate' surge up and with them love and hate between men who had not yet decided on their feelings. He knows that words, as Brice-Parrain says, are 'loaded pistols'. If he speaks, he fires. He may be silent, but since he has chosen to fire he must do it like a man, by aiming at targets, and not like a child, at random, by shutting his eyes and firing merely for the pleasure of hearing the shot go off.(1)

For many children, writing in school, or as Sartre puts it 'firing merely for the pleasure of hearing the shot go off', at the secondary stage becomes rather a pointless activity, and one can understand their attitude. As far as they are concerned, most of them feel that they know how to write, and question the object of regularly producing work which is perhaps more frequently criticised than praised. Fortunately, most children are generous enough to assume that even if they don't know the reasons for their endless activity, the teacher is fully aware of its purpose. Their trust is very touching although I wonder if English teachers really deserve their confidence. Of course, it is not too difficult, given a few minutes of thought, to produce what seem to be convincing explanations for demanding that children write, such as 'It enables them to sort out their ideas and present them in the coherent and structured style which writing demands', or, as followers of David Holbrook might put it, 'In their creative writing they can externalise their own interior conflicts and by means of dramatisation and projection come to some kind of resolution . . .' Incidentally, the problem with the second kind of rationale is that any piece of writing contains not one but two psychological contents: that of the child who writes and that of the teacher who reads what has been written. There are also the more explicitly 'functional' explanations which ultimately legitimise the work of the school: that so many pieces of written work are required for the course work component of an external examination, or that lack of literary skills will handicap the child in the employment market.

I personally don't find any of the above arguments totally convincing and I am sure that were we to confide in the children we teach that these were some of the reasons for their activity, they could, without too much difficulty, find fault with all of them. They could argue, for example, that they are quite capable of discussing ideas without needing to write about them; that the teacher has no right, and is most probably not qualified, to 'psychologise' about the stories and poems that they write; that the Certificate of Secondary Education examination is irrelevant to many of them and is a very arbitrary reason for writing, and that the job they are intended for does not even demand that they think, let alone write.

I think that much of our uncertainty about this issue arises very clearly from the areas of discrepancy between the study and the teaching of English. Teachers study English either at a college of education or at a university, in both cases, although perhaps slightly less so at the former, the content of the course if almost entirely devoted to literary appreciation: the study of, by definition, published works of creative writing in a number of different literary forms. There is little or no expectation that the students themselves will write and very little questioning of the whole idea of the distinction between writers and readers (which, since the roles imposed by the economic system, we might equally well call producers and consumers). Similarly, the study of non-literary forms of writing, other uses of literacy, the sociology and history of communications, are all either marginal to or absent from higher education English courses. Have we yet worked out whether there is, in fact, any theoretical difference at all between the kinds of questions and judgements we take to a 'classic' literary text and those we take to a piece of writing produced in an English lesson?

(A brief autobiographical note: during my five years as a grammar school pupil, from which I escaped twelve years ago, it was never once suggested that the boys in our class could write poems. We naturally assumed that poetry was written by rather effete, and certainly eccentric people with names like Tennyson, Browning and Rupert Brooke. We have come some way since then, but for many of us it is still difficult to break away from our traditional ideas about literary production, so that we can begin to think of the children we teach not only as writers, but as authors.)

Now obviously, the deep study of literature is highly relevant to much of our motivation and sympathy for writing when we are in the classroom. And while we are on teaching practice, using the ideas about how to stimulate the children to write which are generated in the 'professional courses' we undertake, we find that the children are very responsive to our efforts. Unfortunately, the 'stimulus-response' model of English teaching, while sustaining us during a short period of teaching practice, seems unacceptable when we are faced with the prospect of five years' work in English in the secondary school. One begins to realise this when one overhears a boy, walking across the playground as the snow begins to fall, turn to his friends, due to be taught

English next lesson, and say, in a deliberately loud whisper, 'Oh, I suppose we'll have to write a poem about being out in the snow!' The model is, in the end, unacceptable because it is a tautology; it is self-rationalising and ignores the question we started with: why should children write?

I think that we can answer that question with regard to younger children by saying that they write because they enjoy it as an end in itself: 'Firing merely for the pleasure of hearing the shot go off.' Very young children are fascinated with words and enjoy making (and illustrating) stories of fantasy and adventure. There is also the important source of motivation with primary school children that arises from the relatively high 'significance' of the class teacher for whom the work is written. This factor is considerably weakened in the secondary school where the pupil only sees the teacher for perhaps two or three hours a week and often for only one year, when he or she is replaced by another English teacher.

In the secondary school, particularly from the third form upwards, there is a much more frequent resistance to writing, and often the students' arguments, if we acknowledge them, are not without foundation. They realise that their writing situation is a very artificial one, and even if they are only writing for the teacher they often realise that their story or poem will not get the sympathetic attention it deserves because a teacher teaching six classes a week will, theoretically, be reading and marking at least one hundred and eighty other stories, essays and poems as well. Faced with this situation I think we must completely open up the discussion and take a new look at hitherto accepted views of motivation, reason for writing, class-cultural attitudes towards knowledge and the sociology of literary and cultural production.

The dominant debate in education today centres on the question: why do so many working-class children fail in school? Much of the debate focuses on issues which are of particular importance to English teachers: language and culture. The argument about language now almost exclusively takes its bearings from the theoretical models offered by Bernstein. However, quite different perspectives are now being proposed by, for instance, Harold Rosen in this country, who asks for a more thorough understanding of the historical dimension to the variety of working-class cultures that still to some extent shape and consolidate structures of attitudes and feelings.(2)

Two misconceptions about 'the working class' continue to obscure and divert the debate on 'educability': the first is that the working class is an undifferentiated mass with a mechanically controlled set of cultural responses, and the second is that working-class cultures have always been almost exclusively oral. With regard to the first point there are the depressing findings of Goodacre(3) concerning the inability of many teachers to make any valid inferences about children based on parental occupation, and the general ignorance of teachers about degrees of skill and responsibility within working-class occupations. Secondly, we probably need to remind ourselves that during certain periods of our history working-class people were quite capable of producing highly literate responses in political affairs, and of reading and understanding works of theory that would tax many of us teachers today. It is appropriate to note that most social historians date the beginnings of the radical working-class movement from the formation of the London Corresponding Society, a group of mostly skilled artisans concerned with the propagation of radical ideals by means of debate, correspondence and pamphleteering. In 1817 Cobbett's *2d Register* was selling between 40,000 and 60,000 a week, whereas the circulation of the leading daily, *The Times,* during the same period was between 5,000 and 6,000. Between

1791 and 1793 Thomas Paine's *Rights of Man* had sold 200,000 copies in a population of ten million. It would be more true to say that there was a conscious move by the ruling class to divert the working class away from serious reading and written propaganda, towards the passive consumption of diversionary reading.

Radical writers continued to expand the public, John Wade's *Black Book* selling 10,000 an issue, and Cobbett's *Address to the Journeymen and Labourers* selling 200,000 in two months. But it was here, precisely, that active measures were taken against the expansion on the grounds of *the political dangers of too widespread reading*. The heavy taxation of newspapers was supplemented by a series of prosecutions aimed at killing the whole radical press. A different response to the same danger was the development of cheap tracts, of an 'improving kind', designed to counter the success of Cobbett and others, and these were heavily subsidised in this first stage.(4)

What I think one can generalise from history, because there have been many other periods of intense working-class organisation and self-education, is that within working-class cultures, reading and writing have been foremost social activities, shared activities that have not been seen as ends in themselves but as genuine means of communication between men towards an understanding of common problems and mutual enlightenment. And again I think one can generalise also by saying that within certain kinds of middle-class cultural settings, particularly literary and educational ones, reading and writing have been regarded as being ends in themselves, without necessarily any 'functional' overtones. The extreme example of this latter kind of attitude is the allegedly true story of an Oxford college reunion at which the toast was, 'To pure mathematics: may it never be of any use to anyone!' The culture behind such an attitude would, of course, be incomprehensible within any kind of working-class framework. Yet I think that in much of our English teaching we, with some uncertainty perhaps, find the 'non-functional' approach to reading and writing closer to our own intellectual position than what we assume to be its opposite: presumably lots of spelling, letter-writing practice and comprehension exercises on newspaper articles. In actual practice many of us pretend to solve the situation by doing both. I believe, though, that there is an alternative to the highly individualistic 'self-expression' approach, advocated by probably the majority of English teachers at present, which is not at all functional to the employment market but is potentially far more liberating and creative than much of our work at present.

I suggested at the beginning that for many of our students writing for its own sake seemed irrelevant. And I think that that kind of attitude is closely connected with class in that what essentially defines class is the relationship with the means of production. In economic theory, and in fact, the working class are the producers and this is very much a determinant of cultural attitudes as well as occupational ones. In our education system, almost right up to post-graduate level, education is essentially non-productive, and it might be that this feature rather than any other is the source of the 'clash of cultures/values' that most of our sociologists talk about. I think that what we now have to consider, as a matter of real urgency, is how English teaching transforms itself from essentially individualistic and reflective activity into a form of cultural production for others. That is, that we begin to think in terms of the work we do having some social and cultural purpose that goes beyond the confines of the classroom walls.

What makes this situation now possible, to an extent that has not previously been envisaged, is the accessibility of schools to the new reprographic technology. This is not the place to raise the question of the relationship between technology and the new kinds of cultural forms that it makes possible, except to say that in this country we have never really taken the theories and practical possibilities seriously. Again I think teachers in general, and perhaps English teachers in particular, have fought shy of contact with technology, which they often regard with suspicion, or have simply seen it as a helpful aid which enables them to do the old things more easily. The case is, though, and this may seen paradoxical, that the new media technology is potentially much more democratic and amenable to local and individual control than older methods of communication. The move from letterpress printing to photo-lithography provides an appropriate example. With letterpress printing one had to have, to start with, a very expensive composing machine as well as a highly skilled compositor. Each letter of print was cast in an expensive and very heavy metal alloy. Consequently, book production overheads were high, and the addition of illustrations in the form of block engravings made the production of printed material expensive except for books with potentially high sales. Also, once a book had been printed one was faced with the problem of storing all the printing blocks at great expense, or melting them down again in which case reprinting became impossible. With photo-lithography, the image can be produced on a typewriter and then photographed. The photographic negatives can be stored very easily and used again as desired. Illustrations present no separate problem except that they may have to be converted into 'half-tones', which is a simple process. Photo-lithography also means that the author is in control of layout and design since the original art work becomes the photographic plate, whereas with letterpess there was no such flexibility. Today, there are schools which possess their own offset duplicator which can print on hard glossy paper copies of a child's original writing and illustrations.

We have, then, the technological potential now to abolish completely the traditional distinction between writers and readers (producers and consumers), providing we ourselves are prepared to re-think our notion of literary production. It is not simply that one wants to make such changes on wholly theoretical grounds; we have to realise that it is the present system of, in this case, children's book production that is based on an outdated and elitist conception of literary production. A modern trend in children's readers provides an exemplary case. We are now finding, in the commercial publishers' lists, reading schemes which 'are directly relevant to the modern urban working-class child', with breathless titles such as (I characterise) *The Jesmond Alley Crew go Mugging.* In many cases the contents of such readers are very crude and false projections of working-class life, written without empathy or imagination. One wants to ask, surely, 'If you want a direct and true account of everyday life in a city-centre tower block, why not ask a child who lives in one to write it?' At this point we in fact confront that peculiar ideological and mental block which cannot possibly conceive of democratising the process of literary production. I believe that we teachers have to begin to start this process ourselves. It might now be relevant to discuss some of the projects that different children, parents and teachers have been working on in Hackney which provide an idea of how this theory can work very well in practice.

Our first production was a children's reading book, illustrated by photographs, which used a story-line set very specifically in Hackney. This was done with the help of a friend who lived in the area, a very good amateur photographer with a professional understanding of printing processes. The four main characters in the book were played by four first-form boys from the school where I teach. To start with, we outlined a story, which was endorsed by the boys taking part, and then during the days of a half-term holiday took a series of photographs on location which matched the sequence of the story. Once we had developed and printed the photographs, we wrote out the narrative in full and again had this ratified by the boys as to its imaginative authenticity. The story was then sent to be typeset and when we received that back we were able to lay out the book exactly as we wanted. The cost of producing *Hackney Half-Term Adventure*—the title was a compromise of sorts—was £300 for 3,000 copies, which retail at 20p each, of which 1,200 copies have been sold so far in the ten months since it was published. Distribution for the book has been almost completely handled by a local bookshop/community centre, although several local newsagents were persuaded to sell it.

In retrospect, I think that the book would have had more vitality had it been written by the children. However, as it is, it has been enthusiastically read by local children who quickly recognise the location of the photographs as being ones that are familiar to them.

During a discussion with a fourth-form English class about children's reading books they made very much the same kinds of criticisms that many teachers would make: that the settings are remote, mainly rural; that the characters are even more remote, the ubiquitous genteel middle-class, pre-war family of boy, girl, mother, father and faithful dog, Rover, and the language within the books inert and inconsequential. It then seemed obvious to ask them to produce books themselves which could be used by younger boys within the school. Since we have a number of cheap cameras in the English department, they were also able to illustrate their stories. Two groups of boys chose to make books as single assignments for their CSE course work folder. Knowing that the book was intended for younger boys, each group 'borrowed' two boys who then became the central characters in the stories. Both groups planned their books in terms of the camera shots that they wanted to take and once this was settled they went out for the morning, under supervision, with the younger boys and took their photographs. The settings they chose were mainly the favourite play sites used by the boys themselves: by the canal and on the marshes. After the photographs had been printed they worked on their groups, and after a few lessons each group produced a collectively written text to accompany the photographs. The books were then duplicated with stencils cut on an electronic stencil cutter which permits the reproduction of photographs. The end products, although perhaps rather crude by commercial standards, were very well received by the younger children.

One of the most important features of this idea is that the language and syntax used in the books are precisely those used by the children themselves: their key words rather than ours. There is also the fact that because the younger, less enthusiastic readers themselves become the characters in the stories, there is the maximum possible identification, and this is obviously very closely linked with motivation. Another crucial difference between this kind of local, democratic process of book production and that of the commercial publishers is that this kind of reading book not only benefits the readers but there is also the very important educational and social experience involved in the production. New ways of working together and planning are involved and an interest is developed in picture composition, layout and writing within a new kind of context. The concept of authorship begins to lose its traditional aura and the activity of writing acquires a genuine social purpose; the pupils are genuinely helping each other.

Obviously this process is apposite to 'the great reading problem'. Although we now seem to be preoccupied with scientific models for the teaching of reading skills, it is very probable that the important questions of motivation and cultural relevance required in wanting to learn to read have been relegated to a rather insignificant position.

In the past year a number of new titles have been added to the English department stocklist: *The Soldier's Story*, written by a fourth-form boy and illustrated by one of his classmates; *The Red Bus and Other Stories* by six boys from one first-year class; *My Best Friend*, two longer stories by two other first-form boys: *Vivian Usherwood: Poems*, now also available in a glossy printed public version, and others are in the process of production. It is not too difficult to imagine the situation, a highly desirable one, I believe, in which most of the reading material available within a school would in fact be produced by the children themselves and other members of the community. This is not to propose that the very good, commercially published books by many of the better children's writers should not be used, but the community-produced books could well replace much of the 'hack' material that schools at present are forced to use because of the lack of an alternative. In many cases, though, we are filling gaps which the commercial publishers have never tried to tackle, particularly with very short stories for the slow readers who are nowhere near Alan Garner, John Rowe Townsend, Philippa Pearce and others. One is also breaking down the mysterious aura that books have for many children by presenting them with material that has been written by their own friends, and not by some faraway author whose books can seem a form of mental intimidation.

In our own case a school publishing programme would certainly be assisted by better reprographic material—we need now, I believe, an offset duplicator and a plate-maker—but most schools should be able to get access to better equipment through a resources centre or a teachers' centre.

Outside our particular school similar proejcts are now happening. We have recently produced a collection of social and historical documents about Hackney called *If it wasn't for the houses in between . . .* which has been designed like a 'Jackdaw' and contains a selection of historical maps, photographs, extracts from locally based novels, copies of local General Strike newspapers, a selected glossary of cockney slang and transcripts of tapes made with older members of the community.

Two other larger projects are planned for production by the middle of the year. The first is to be a sequel to the history pack which will look at Hackney from the beginning of the Second World War up until the end of the century. It will include transcripts of interviews made by schoolchildren with local people, including their parents, about what it was like to live in Hackney during the war: effects on family relationships, work done, questions of community feeling, and so on. It will also use interviews made with local people living in high-rise flats, as well as other kinds of housing situations, with comments by the children themselves. Also, local interest groups, such as tenants' associations, playgroup organisations, trade unions, residents' associations, local authority sub-committees, amenity groups, etc., will be asked to write about and be interviewed about their own recommendations, hopes and fears for the quality of life in the future Hackney. As much as possible of this recording work, as well as layout and design, will be done by schoolchildren.

The second major project involves the production of a paperback book containing four local autobiographies. This has arisen out of a Hackney WEA class which has been working on a course entitled 'A People's Autobiography of Hackney'. So far about twelve lengthy tape-recordings have been made with local people, asking them to talk about their lives. At least two of the tapes, one made with a clerk who left school in 1912 at the age of fourteen, and who for frequent periods of his life was unemployed, the other made with a seventy-two-year-old ex-shoemaker who talks about learning the trade from his grandfather, are more than three hours long and immensely vivid and fascinating accounts of life in the past. Such transcripts will form the published autobiographies which, again, will probably be of considerable use in schools. But, also one is enabling the community to become conscious of itself by the flexibility of the means of communication now available. There is so much knowledge, so much creative ability, that has so long been ignored, within any community, that can now become public as part of a completely new kind of educational process of people talking and writing and illustrating for each other, quite independent of the legitimised forms of public communication.

Which is why we must become aware of the opportunities made available to us by the new technology, and acquaint ourselves with its workings and educational possibilities. There is not time here to mention other kinds of possibilities of communication on a local basis which cassette tape-recorders, video-tape cameras and play-back machines, as well as other technological developments, offer us. They exist and demand to be utilised.

These ideas are not original; the possibilities that the new media technology makes available in terms of democratising the cultural process have frequently been considered in other countries—certainly more so than in Britain.(5) Our efforts to work along these lines in English teaching will be complemented by similar developments elsewhere in the curriculum: I am thinking of the move towards community service in the upper school, of the idea of utilising elementary scientific knowledge in the interests of the community by making ecological studies of the local environment (testing different kinds of local pollution) that now take place in a number of schools. English teachers can make themselves central to this process by the ways in which their work becomes available to the wider audience. This could start, and the English departments in a number of Hackney schools have worked together on this, by persuading the local newspaper to regularly feature children's work. It could then go beyond that point by the production within and between schools of books of stories, poems and discursive essays in which children begin to write for others. Eventually there is the wider readership of the whole community, who themselves can produce for the children.

At present our system of education is based on the idea of the children as passive consumers of knowledge which perhaps prepares them too neatly for their adult functions as consumers of material and cultural production. We perform a disservice to the children we teach if we confirm them in their roles as consumers only, or, by practice, never suggest that their writing is anything more than 'self-expression'. In short, they must become authors, and we have to locate their audience, and to make available to them the means of production.

References

1 Jean-Paul Sartre, *What is Literature,* Methuen, 1950.
2 H. Rosen, *Language and Class,* Falling Wall Press, 1972.
3 E.J. Goodacre, *Teachers and their Pupils' Home Background,* NFER, 1968.
4 Raymond Williams, *The Long Revolution,* Chatto & Windus, 1961; Penguin 1965, p.186. My italics.
5 The ideas in this essay have been strongly influenced by the writings of Walter Benjamin. Two of his essays in particular are appropriate to the argument: 'The work of art in an age of mechanical reproduction', in *Illuminations,* Cape, 1970; and 'The author as producer', *New Left Review,* no.62, 1970. A writer who devoted a great deal to the potentialities of the book was El Lissitzky, whose essay 'The book' is available in *El Lissitzky: Life—Letters—Texts,* Thames & Hudson, 1968. For the debate on relationships between the media and technology and the democratisation of culture, one recent essay seems to me to be outstanding: Hans Magnus Enzensberger, 'Constituents of a theory of the media', *New Left Review,* no.64, 1970.

Further Reading

The following suggestions for further reading are all books that seem to me, in different ways, to tackle the main issues that I have tried to outline in my essay. Central to those issues in the problem of cultural democracy.

W. Benjamin, *Illuminations: Essays and Reflections,* Cape, 1970.

J. Berger, *A Fortunate Man,* Writers and Readers Publishing Cooperative, 1976.

William Morris, *News from Nowhere,* 1891 (Routledge, 1970).

R. Williams, *Culture and Society,* Chatto & Windus, 1958; Penguin 1961.

The Long Revolution, Chatto & Windus, 1961; Penguin, 1965.

E.P. Thompson, *The Making of the English Working Class* Gollancz, 1963; Penguin, 1968.

School of Barbiana, *Letter to a Teacher,* Penguin, 1970.

Two poems on inequality
*Christine Reed**

1. What are Words Really for?

In Vietnam a little child died
But we couldn't decide the paper for the living-room
And in Canning Town an old lady cried
So lonely inside all alone in her sitting-room
And the bishops in Rome, that great christian home
Still had to decide should the priests stay celibate
While in Belfast, the soldiers rush past another bomb blast
No feeling inside, no time to hesitate
Each man must decide why a little child died
And some mother cried by the ruins of her humble home
What are words really for?
Can we ever be sure we're not praying in vain for a new
   world again?

2. A Lesson in History

There's a lesson in Tutankamun
Worshipping gold as a beautiful thing
A thousand slaves sacrificed
In the name of one important king
The useless use of people
That one mighty man may obtain
His little piece of Heaven
Wasn't worth one drop of rain
But still we marvel at precious gold
At the greed we may attain
We should grieve to see worn, torn Vietnam

*A secondary school student

Worship the gold in a field of grain
And we still make a man important
And place him on a throne
And fill our heads with self-importance
And all the things we own
What a lesson in Tutankamun
If we use our hearts to see
And close our eyes to all the gold
A lesson in history.

Out There or Where the Masons Went

Harold Rosen

'Not knowing the people, they are like heroes without a battlefield . . . What do they not understand? The language.'
Mao-Tse-Tung (1)

So we are going to talk about the social context? And a good thing too. But strange. The tidy abstraction of it; a non-combative, dusted-down, orderly little phrase. What does it stand for? The little world we can look at through the window, go shopping in, take buses from, play truant in? The invisible hinterland of this morning's *Times* where I read of 'the magnification of state benefits as the major source of subsistence for unproductive members of society'? The portable 'construction of reality', the internal architecture we have built for ourselves out of our social encounters? It cannot be the ramshackle edifice of institutions, pronouncements, channels of communication, labelled strata, laws and doctrines cobbled together by history for us to scuttle about in. The social context, as we call it, is not an arena in which we perform our dramas. It is the dramas themselves; people in action with each other and against each other improvising the text as they proceed.

'Thus it is not language which generates what people say. Language does not possess this magical power or possesses it only fitfully and dubiously. What people say derives from praxis from the performance of tasks, from the division of labour— arises out of real actions, real struggles in the world. What they actually do, however, enters consciousness only by way of language, by being said.'(2)

Therefore, if I am a bit needled by the phrase, 'the social context', it is because, cropping up like this, it announces that we are moving on to our next interesting theme and in due course we shall proceed to others. But that isn't it at all. Essentially, *there is nothing else to talk about.*

And we have talked about it. When we have, it has turned out to be not a fastidious excursion into the streets, not an awestruck promenade round our minds, not a jolly linguistic field trip (though it often starts in these ways) but a battlefield on which the lines are being more and more clearly delineated. It is becoming increasingly difficult to refuse to take sides. We have to choose between descriptions of an impoverished restricted code and the unearthing of a living oral tradition, between visions of school as a civilized and well-ordered island in a sea of barbarism and anomie and the aspiration that they should be reincarnate through the nourishment of the neighbourhood and community, between reading 'schemes' and literacy through critical consciousness (Freire).[3] Indeed all the choices we make, minute, urgent, even trivial, are more and more seen as taking sides. English teaching has become overtly a political matter. Chris Searle can be heard demanding passionately 'reciprocity, comradeship, shared experience'[4] against the amplified phantasmagora of Sir Keith Joseph, making our flesh creep with the teeming illegitimates spawned by the plebs, calling for a return to the old orderly ways.

It is out of assumptions about the nature of our society that new ways of English teaching have grown and changed. One old new way is for the teacher to open the eyes of his gullible pupils to the seductions of mass-media and advertising. Himself immune (by what process of innoculation?), he will give immunity to others. He assumes that all around him the most baleful cultural forces of our society work fully and effectively and that only his critically-trained perceptions pick up the nuances of the non-stop confidence trick. Yet Raymond Williams showed us years ago the great difference between what people *make* of television and what they are expected to make of it. The banner-bearers of the High Culture have been telling us for so long that 'mass' culture is debased and fraudulent and sterile. Nevertheless the cankers have got at their own confidence.

> Our dried voices when
> We whisper together
> Are quiet and meaningless
> As wind in dry grass
> Or rats' feet over broken glass
> In our dry cellar.
> > T.S. Eliot(5)

Our voices? Take this one which Connie Rosen(6) collected from a school in Birmingham, an ordinary voice,

> This ordinary woman
> Works in the factory up the road
> Putting bolts in the drill
> She presses the pedal that starts the drill working
> The clashing and the grinding
> The clicking and the shuttling
> Are soothing to her ears
> Filling her arms with rhythm
> Her head with day-dreams.
> The siren sound
> And my mother faces the world again.

The doleful litany chanted endlessly is that the children and young people in schools are totally submerged by powerful manipulative forces outside their control which brutalize and stupefy them. If that message strikes home then it is small wonder if teachers who step forward to expose, analyse and demolish, feel in their hearts that they are puny in the face of giants who can spend more on one advertisement than one of them will spend on school books in the whole of a teaching career.

Of course it is right to see and understand how such things work but the mistake is to believe that all around us are nothing but sad and spiritless victims. There are other forces at work. The miracle is not that we are all deformed by the dominant culture of our society but how much grows in the teeth of it, how our humanity asserts itself, how it asserts itself in the world of our pupils. We should not see the tabloids and commercials as the only emblems of their world, just as we should refuse to let a sanctified canon of literary works be the only alternative voice.

For there is that other assumption about society which corrodes our thinking, that the great working-class of this country with its largely unwritten history, its heroism, its self-transforming engagement with life, its stubborn refusal to be put down is nothing but a deprived inarticulate herd. Even the new radical teacher sensitive to the language of working-class pupils and armed with political theory can be corroded by the social assumptions which abound in current educational and sociological literature. We are told that working-class children cannot learn to read because they have no books in the home and their parents do not read. Transmitted deprivation I believe they call it now. Yet millions of people throughout Europe in the late nineteenth and early twentieth centuries won their way to literacy from homes which were totally illiterate. Theories about the cycle of deprivation, glibly cited by politicians, have lurking beneath their surface an unhistorical notion that generations passively reproduce cultural attitudes; long before the 1870 Act, in 1844 Engels(7) showed that, from from amidst conditions of appalling squalor and exploitation, workers were producing a literary culture of their own

'They have translated the French materialists, Helvetius, Holback, Diderot, etc. and disseminated them, with the best

English works, in cheap editions. Strauss' *Life of Jesus* and Proudhon's *Property* circulate among working men only. Shelley, the genius, the prophet Shelley, and Byron, with his glowing sensuality and his bitter satire upon our existing society, find most of their readers in the proletariat; the bourgeoisie owns only castrated editions . . . .'

Turn to David Craig's magnificent book *The Real Foundations: Literature and Social Change,*(8) which is so much more than literary criticism, and you will find the careful documentation and interpretation of changes in working-class consciousness, imagination and culture over more than a century and a half.

Teachers who have peered over the school wall and are intensely aware of 'out there' find themselves caught in a tormenting paradox and heart-breaking decisions. They see that most of their pupils are bound for jobs which are destructive of the spirit, that they will be working in conditions which are a denial of initiative, imagination, and participation. And yet all their teaching has been designed to foster personal sensitivity, personal response and self-exploration. Thus there are only intolerable choices. Prepare them for boredom and docility (euphemized into 'preparing them for society') or have them jettison all the work of the school years as soon as they perceive its irrelevance to their situation. But there are several flaws in the picture. Our own location in society and our own formation lead us to see only three forces at work—the grinding and destructive power of brutalizing jobs, the downward pull of bookless homes and philistine communities ranged against our informed wisdom. Whatever we have gained from our education, what it is least likely to have given us is a confident belief that there is any nourishing resource and vigour in the pupils' homes and community and that we have much to learn from that community. Perhaps, in the necessary emphasis we have given to *personal* growth, language for *personal* development and literature as an intensely *personal* exploration we have made English sound like the greatest ego-trip ever invented and we have forgotten that when working-class children have responded to our teaching then it is either because we have lured them into a world of private experience and cushioned individualism or because we have seen them as socially constituted human beings who can draw sustenance for the imagination from their own world and its values, from parents, grandparents and neighbours. I believe the best of new English teaching has been of the second kind. Ken Worpole(9) has shown through the work of Centerprise and *A People's Autobiography of Hackney* what kinds of responses are nurtured and evoked in places which seem from the outside either silent and subdued or centres of degrading violence.

Few of us have seen English as a training in conducting inaccessible dialogues with the self. We have sensed the health in uninterrupted transactions between private experience and social experience but we have lacked a sufficient understanding of the social consciousness of our pupils. So much has already been achieved by pioneering English teaching, but if it is to take, to bite deep then we must engage with working-class life and learn to apply our educated ears to its voice, with the same respect, awareness of nuances and human warmth we have applied so readily elsewhere. This is really the next bold step for English teaching. And it takes a lot of courage: for it means shifting our centre of gravity away from the usual sources of confirmation and approval. This is the shift that Chris Searle (10) has made. He quotes Mazine, aged 13,

> All living in one community
> Thinking for each other
> Helping each other
> No betrayals . . .

and comments

The English teacher in the schools is probably in the best position to give back to the child his own world and identity in education, to re-affirm it, to share it himself, support it and strengthen it.

Chris Searle is concerned with working-class identity not with how to create an individual awareness so frail it will melt in the heat of the production line.

One of the most deeply rooted ideas among us is that working-class life is a miserable and squalid affair unredeemed by delicate joys and sorrow, devoid of deep understanding and bold aspirations. I am not speaking of that suburban squeamishness which fears and hates every form of working-class assertion from the bold, shameless voices and noisy laughter to the nasty tendency to act together in defiance of established power. Nor am I speaking of the way in which the ruling class knows its enemy and manages to despise it, fear it and attack it. What I am speaking of is that tendency in progressive opinion of all kinds, including all kinds of socialists, to see working-class life as a horrifying ulcer springing from the unwholesomeness of capitalist society, a deforming disease which a new and better society would purge and cleanse.

> 'Ever since industrialism took over, writers in the vein of Ruskin and William Morris have either argued from the physical ugliness, the blight of spoiled ground and sprawl of unplanned jerry-building, to the feelings of the people themselves, not seeing that human beings have extraordinary powers of resistance and enjoyment; or else they have taken a disgusted line about modern human nature itself and supposed that our actual capacity for experience has been weakened since the good old days (whenever they were).'
>
> D. Craig(11)

The alternative view amounts to this, that out there in the 'social context' there is a culture which is alive and kicking. Just as we have discovered that children do not come to school to be given language but arrive with it as a going concern, we need to discover that children come with this too. Indeed, their language, the despised vernacular of great cities and industrial towns, is part of it.

I do not think this means a sentimental vicarious undiscriminating adoration of everything which takes root in working-class communities, any more than I believe that it means the rejection of everything our own education has taught us. But the disentangling and sorting has still to be done. This is one of the huge tasks ahead of us—a vast re-learning and an application of responses refined in the study of poetry and novels to everyday speech.

I might have begun in another place. Let me spend a little time there. Suppose I tell you that there is a little-known story of D.H. Lawrence, which contains this,

> Well, when my poor ole pot and pan were working, were working at Tickleton Main—ooh it were a deep pit you know. They used to come out wringing wet, their trammin' drawers you know. I've seen him slosh it on floor and it's sloshed down like a dirty old floor cloth. I've had to swill em out, swill em, swill coal dust off them and dry them before he went to work next day. His pocket which he brought his tramming drawers home in and his belt which used to fasten his trammin   drawers to 'im when he was trammin—he weren't in good health and I know he was on nights—I had nightmares occasionally.
> When aught depresses me I always have a nice little nightmare to myself and I know this night I didn't—I had Leonard's mother with me, you know, for twenty years—after dad died, after her husband died and she were in t'other room and she said,
> 'Amy, what couldn't you sleep through t'night?'
> I says, 'Eh, why?'
> She says, 'You did sing.'
> I says, 'Did I?'
> 'I heard somebody singing,' she says, 'Well, you were singing.'
> She said, 'A' for what you're singing?'
> 'Well,' I says, 'It weren't me, Gran, it weren't me.'
> 'It were you what were singing.'

I tell you and I felt—and I said, 'were it this.'
(Sings)
　　For he toils down that mine, down that dark dreary pit,
　　So that folks like us round the fireside will cheer.
　　And he toils down below far from heaven's glorious light
　　And his face may be black but his big heart is white.
I says, 'Was that it?'
'Aye', she says, 'that were it.'
I says, 'Oh my God.' I said, 'No it's never come to that.
I'm singing in my sleep because I'm upset about his work.'
But it must have been me because she said, 'That were t'song.
That were it I heard you singing.'

How did you read that? What kind of careful, reverent
attention did you give it? What can you say about its
dialogue, its shaped utterance, its sense of felt life and so
on? But now read it again but bear in mind that it is in
fact not by D.H. Lawrence but is the spontaneous
language of a Yorkshire miner's wife which appears in
Language and Class Workshop, No. 2.(12) Charles Parker
recorded it and it came *not* in response to a request for a
story or autobiography but to his request for old songs. I
might have chosen other items from the collection, West
Indian children telling traditional stories, miner's jokes,
political fables, working women from Manchester and
Liverpool finding fluent and powerful language as they
become involved in controlling their own lives, and
working men and women giving their complex views
about language. Give material like this the same loving
attention you have lavished on literature and you will
extend your humanity. It is not a matter of asserting that
working-class culture is infinitely superior. (Who
suggested that anyway? Where? When?) but rather of
demonstrating that it is there at all, that it is pertinent to
our concerns, that we build on it or build nothing.

'In the evening when the Chinese Wall was finished
Where did the masons go? . . . .'
Bertolt Brecht

References

1 Mao-Tse-Tung. *Problems of art and literature,* International Publishers, 1950.
2 H. Lefebvre, *The Sociology of Marx,* Allen Lane, 1968.
3 P. Freire, *Education for critical consciousness,* Sheed and Ward, 1974. *Education: The Practice of Freedom* Writers and Readers Publishing Cooperative 1976.
4 C. Searle, *This new season,* Calder and Bryars, 1973.
5 T.S. Eliot, *Collected Poems, 1909-1935,* Faber and Faber, 1936.
6 C. Rosen and H. Rosen, *The language of primary school children,* Penguin, 1973.
7 F. Engels, *Condition of the working-class in 1844.*
8 D. Craig, *The real foundations: literature and social change,* Chatto and Windus, 1972.
9 K. Worpole, 'The School and the community' in *Education or domination,* ed. Holly, D., Arrow, 1974.
10 C. Searle, op.cit.
11 D. Craig, op.cit.
12 Language and class workshop, No. 2, Nov. 1974 ed. H. Rosen (41a Muswell Ave., N10 2EH).

Acknowledgements

Part of the article 'The History and Politics of Literacy' first appeared in *Radical Education* No. 1 1974. Quintin Hoare's article is from *New Left Review*, Vol 32, 1967. The Engels extract is from *The Condition of the Working Class in England*, Panther 1969; and the Trotsky extract from *On Literature and Art*, Pathfinder 1970. Wayne O'Neil's 'Properly Literate' was originally published in the *Harvard Educational Review*, Vol. 40, No. 2, 1970. Camilla Nightingale's article is from *West One;* and Kristine Falco's appears in *Women on the Move*, edited by Leppaluoto J.R. Know Inc. 1973. 'All Things White and Beautiful' is an extract from an article which was published in *Hard Cheese*, No.3, 1974; and which appears in full in Bob Dixon's *Catching Them Young* Vol. I *Sex, Race and Class in Children's Fiction*, Pluto Press 1977; and Daniel Kunene's 'African Vernacular Writing' is taken from a longer article in *African Social Research*, No. 9, 1970. Ken Worpole's 'Beyond the Classroom Walls' appears as 'Beyond Self-Expression: English and the Community' in *New Movements in the Study and Teaching of English*, published by Temple Smith 1973; and Harold Rosen's article comes from *English in Education*, Vol. 9, No. 1, 1975.

... other titles from Writers & Readers

Available from bookshops or direct from
Writers and Readers Publishing Cooperative
14 Talacre Road, London NW5 3PE

p/b 45p
ISBN 0 904613 30 5

p/b 35p
ISBN 0 904613 36 4

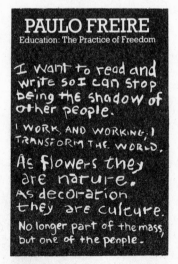

p/b £1.00
ISBN 0 904613 16 X

p/b £1.00
ISBN 0 904613 31 3

The World in a Classroom
Compiled by Chris Searle

p/b £1.95
ISBN 0 904613 46 1
h/b £4.95
ISBN 0 904613 45 3

CLASSROOMS OF RESISTANCE

COMPILED BY CHRIS SEARLE

p/b 85p
ISBN 0 904613 01 1
h/b £2.75
ISBN 0 904613 10 0

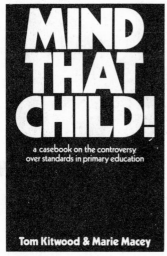

MIND THAT CHILD!

a casebook on the controversy over standards in primary education

Tom Kitwood & Marie Macey

p/b 65p
ISBN 0 094613 44 5

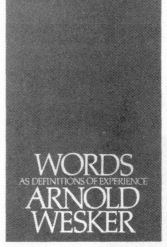

WORDS
AS DEFINITIONS OF EXPERIENCE
ARNOLD WESKER

p/b 75p
ISBN 0 904613 26 7